The Squirrel Stole My Thong and Other Reasons I'm Still Single

✄

Deirdre Sargent

SWM PRESS
San Francisco

SWM Press
1271 Washington Avenue, #692
San Leandro, CA 94577

This book is a work of satire. While some items are true, some I just plum made up. The names are real or not depending on whether I owe you money, have too much respect for you or you're not speaking to me at the moment. All similarities to people living or dead is purely coincidence.

Produced by SWM Press
ISBN-13: 978-0-9837646-7-0

Manufactured in the United States of America

DEDICATION

This book is dedicated to Kat for being my friend, my inspiration and my guiding light, and to Sam who believed that my writing was worth getting out there.

ACKNOWLEDGMENTS

I want to thank all the members of "The Treehouse", especially Maggie, Scott and Joel for the support. My sister Nadine for being a great editor and not killing me when I couldn't keep my verb tenses straight

Cover Design by Nelly Murariu

Copy Editing by Nadine Asef-Sargent

Author Photo by JoNell Franz

INTRODUCTION

To Begin at the Beginning

San Francisco. The City by the Bay. It's where I was born and where I live. I've moved around in my life but have always gravitated back to the Bay Area with its fog, mild climate and potable water. This is actually an odd choice for a single gal.

New York City is fast-paced, cynical and has lobbied to make chain-smoking an Olympic event. I don't understand New York, or East Coasters for that matter, but the people who live there love it and are very possessive of their city. The women of Manhattan find the men they meet in the parks, the cafes, and the boardrooms irresistible, and good on them, but I just couldn't live that life.

Los Angeles is superficial, plastic and damn proud of it. It's glitz and tits and if you aren't blonde, twenty-three years old, six feet tall, and one hundred twenty pounds, you really shouldn't even bother moving there. I lived in LA for many years but I had to leave. They actually sent me an eviction notice once I passed the one hundred twenty five pound mark. Seriously, I wanted to live in a place where I could breathe the air, drink water out of the tap and not be mocked because I don't look like a Somali orphan.

So I moved back to the San Francisco area. The problem? What is San Francisco known for besides sourdough bread and Dungeness crabs? Well, in case you've been living on Mars for the past forty years and didn't know, it just so happens to be the Mothership of hip, gay culture. That's great if you're a gay man or a lesbian. As a straight woman, well, I've just cut my options down dramatically by moving here.

In spite of everything, I am positive that out there is a fantastic guy who will appreciate me and not mind that I say "penis" at least twice a day. I mean, change happens. Fantastic things happen all the time to people.

So why not to me?

MY BIG FAT GAY CAT

I may not have a man, but I have a cat. Cat seems like such an understated term. He's more like a twenty pound demonic black basketball from Hell.

He came into my life in a round-about way. My housemate at the time, Roxy, killed a black cat on the 4th of July. She didn't mean to. It wasn't like she was gunning for him or anything. We had gone up by Mt. Wilson to watch the fireworks and while driving home, a black cat ran out in front of the car and she hit it. We went back to check on it and it was dead, poor thing. We knocked on doors but couldn't find the owner.

Months later, Roxy heard from an acquaintance at the Burbank Animal Shelter that they had a large black cat up for adoption. She said the man who operated the shelter was a dog person who would let dogs stay as long as they had the room but put cats down after the mandatory waiting period of three to five days.

Roxy thought if I adopted this cat, thus saving its life, I would balance the karmic scales for the cat she killed. I'm not sure how that all works since I wasn't driving the car that killed the cat. Would my sacrifice help pay off her karmic debt to the Universe? I'm not a Buddhist, so I have no idea. However, it did sound like a good plan, so off I went with my friend Susan to check out this cat.

The cat jail at the Burbank Humane Society consisted of rows and rows of stacked cages, containing cats of many shapes and sizes. I decided I wanted a black cat with green eyes, and he had to be of substantial size. I didn't want a Nicole Ritchie lookin' cat, I wanted a robust Queen Latifah cat.

We looked at many cats. Small cats, fluffy cats, cats that did tricks. "They're trying too hard," was Susan's observation of the possible contenders. At last we reached a cage containing a cat whose bulk nearly filled the space. He had a large square head, amber eyes, was a bit dusty and squatted there like a huge meatloaf. He just didn't seem to give a shit. The tag on his cage proclaimed his name was Chucky and his owners surrendered him because he was peeing all over the house.

The helpful Humane Society gal said they had no way of knowing whether or not the excuse the owners used was true. A great many times, people just make up an excuse so they can pretend they aren't dumping their pet like a disposable bag. This pisses me off. Just for a minute, let's pretend these are all human kids instead of furry kids.

One day you decide you can't stand your spawn anymore, or you're moving and the kid doesn't match the new furniture, or there just isn't room for the kid in the new condo, or the kid barfed on your couch so now you're pissed off. Just picture that...

"We're really sorry but we can't take little Billy with us. Jason has a new job, so we had to move, and the condo doesn't allow children. I'm sure Billy will get a good home." Or "Janie just kept wetting the bed. Beds are expensive, so Janie has to go."

I know, you're saying, "It's not the same thing!" Really? I say it's exactly the same thing. If you make a commitment to a living creature that's dependent on you, then it's for better or worse, not until it gets difficult or you get bored. Oh, you're saying, "Well children are different because they are your own blood." Really?

How about adopted kids or step kids? Are they less worthy of your love and attention because they don't share your DNA? I think not. It's the same thing people, so suck it up.

I decided I would have to think about this because if he really was peeing all over the house, this would be something I would have to deal with for the rest of his natural life. I wanted a day to think about it. Susan liked him. She said he had character.

The cat jail gal said he was on his last day and if I didn't want him he would be put down tomorrow. No pressure or anything. So I left and thought about it. First thing in the morning I called and told her, "Don't kack him! I'm coming down after work to pick him up."

So, I brought a cardboard cat carrier with me. Silly me, I should have brought something stronger, like a rebar enforced cage. You see, when they hefted Mr. Man's bulk into the carrier and I started to walk out with him – flump – he fell out of the bottom of the box. The bottom just gave way under his hefty muscled girth and he splayed frog-like in the middle of the hallway, freaked out and ran back into the cat jail room.

"Hey! Cat! I am trying to save you from certain death!" He wasn't listening. He was too busy hiding under rows of cat cages while the Humane Society guy tried to flush him out by poking at him with a broom. Finally, the cat was recaptured, stuffed into the box again as I held onto the bottom so we didn't have a repeat of the previous escape attempt.

After I paid his bail and piled him into the car, I determined that Chucky was an awful name. Sorry to any Chuckys out there, but ever since that stupid horror movie came out, when I hear the name, all I can picture is a creepy, soulless, maniacal ginger doll with bad fashion sense. I just couldn't do that to my cat, so I renamed him Chauncy. I felt that was a much more dignified name for a cat of his demeanor and substantial size.

Chauncy turned out to be a great cat. He did have territorial issues with other cats and yes, he would spray. I just had to deal with that since I'm not going to kill my kid for wetting the bed. He is huge and in a way more like a dog than a cat. He's also gay.

How do I know he's gay? How do I know my nephew likes Anime or ice cream? It was pretty obvious to everyone. My friends all knew. They kept trying to tell me, and I thought they were giving me a hard time. They kept telling me to embrace my big fat gay cat and to accept him in all his gay glory. I would just respond with, "My cat's not gay!"

Why was I so obstinate? I just didn't see how a cat could be gay. Until I really paid attention. If I had just been honest with myself from the beginning I would have seen that he was just born that way. The only cats he would spend time with, or even tolerate, were male cats. He had no time for female cats at all. No displays, no attempted mating, nothing. They could have been pieces of furniture for all he cared.

The first sign of Chauncy's homosexual inclinations became clear when he met Bob. When we moved to the Bay Area, there was a small, thin cat that lived upstairs from us. Chauncy wasn't much for being outside, but he would sit on the porch. One day I saw him sitting out there next to the svelte black cat. She was very pretty. Chauncy would touch noses with her, lick her, and sit next to her in the sun. One day I ran into the cat's owner. I said, "Looks like Chauncy has a girlfriend. What's your cat's name?" "Bob," she replied. My roomie, Ruth, looked at me with that knowing look of hers and said, "I told you your cat is gay."

After Bob came Horace, and then when we moved from the apartment into this house there was Norton from next door. Chauncy was so upset when Norton moved that he was off his food for a week. I suppose it was obvious if you had the brains to see, and I am fine with that. It doesn't matter to me if Chauncy is gay. It's how he was born and I love my big, fat, gay cat!

If wonder if there's a parade for that?

MY LIFE IS FALLING APART, JUST LIKE MY DECK

There are days when I wonder if I should even bother getting out of bed. I realize there are a great many things I should be grateful for. Let's see, I'm not eating out of a trashcan. That's always good. I'm not living on the street, another plus. I really don't have the wardrobe for street living or Freegan grazing through the trash bins of San Francisco and the greater East Bay.

Why the sudden turn? Why the gloomy outlook on life? It's because I am now unemployed. I had a great job at a large internet company. My life was wonderful. I made good money, I bought my first house. It was a small but darling craftsman with hardwood floors and built-ins. Sure it was tiny but it was mine. I could paint the walls if I felt like it. I could run around starkers if I was in the mood.

My life has gone from great to depressing in two point three seconds. My five-year, high-paying career in the dot.com industry came to a screetching halt. I was laid off in what I now refer to as "the great dot.com implosion of aught three." It just sounds so old fashioned and pretentious that way. I have yet to find another full time job. I now exist on temp jobs and grande non-fat, no water chai lattes from Starbucks.

The fabulous house I bought? The house my accountant said I had to buy? The house I was so excited to get? Well I was laid off three weeks after escrow closed. Again, major suckage. The house was supposed to be an investment against any future financial

7

woes. An opportunity to be a grown adult, have some security towards my retirement and besides, it sounds great when you say "my house" and it really is. You aren't a renter, you're an owner, or at least you pay the mortgage. Now in the blink of an eye, everything has shifted.

I am also still single, which appears to make me a social pariah. I never really thought having a ring would be such a huge deal. It's not like I haven't had offers. Sure I've had offers, anyone can have offers. The real question is do you want to spend your life (or a good chunk of it) with this person? I decided no. Why settle for a polyester jumpsuit when you're sure there is a perfect size eight Betsy Johnson dress out there that will fit you like a glove. Yeah, dream on.

So, I am currently jobless, husbandless and have bought a house that needs a new roof and back porch. Whee! Lucky me. When I was buying the house, the roof passed inspection. It looked fine, until it started to leak like a sieve at the first rain. The back porch is the size of a postage stamp and as rotten as an investment bankers soul. The stairs have been in a state of decay for at least a decade. The middle of the deck is so spongy with rot, it forces me to give the admonition to my friends that I can't have more than four hundred total pounds of weight out on the deck at one time, which puts a hitch in evening parties. I am also seeing a guy I am way too good for but I settled on because I am bored and dumb. Another reason not to leave the safety of my bed.

My big, fat, gay cat Chauncy, stares at me with those glowing amber eyes, full of judgment and recrimination. I can just see him assessing my whiny ass problems and finding them wanting. More importantly, since he does not have opposable thumbs, he is unable to operate the can opener and wants to be fed. Yeah, I can hear him now, "Hey Monkey! Open the can or I will pee in your bookcase!"

Wonderful. I motivate myself to get up and dress in something stylish and hip. Who am I kidding? My current outfit of choice amounts to a pair of too big J. Crew cargo pants, a paint splattered, old denim shirt, and a pair of ratty tennis shoes my Mother has been trying to bin for the past three years. Yes, Tyra Banks would be so proud of my "fierce" look. I snort and look for my chai in its handy white and green Starbucks cup. I am in dire need of fortification for the afternoon project: hauling crap out of the back yard.

Allow me to explain. This piece of shit, rotten, falling down back porch is the current bane of my existence. You have to walk on the left side of the stairs, because if you step on the right, your leg will end up stuck halfway through the rotted wood. The deck itself has a soft spot in the middle that precludes anyone over the size of a German Shepherd from standing on it for any length of time without the risk of plunging twelve feet to the cement below.

Then, along comes my erstwhile boyfriend Carter and my long-suffering friend Paul to help out as I pour on the damsel in distress routine. They tear down the rotten mess and build a brand new, kick-ass back patio deck. You would think this would make me happy, but no, it doesn't. You see, there is a huge metal shed that takes up more than half of my small backyard. The boys have stacked the planks of rotted old deck next to the shed, turning it into one big rotting rat condo. However, once the planks are all gone, I will be able to remove the big shed, leaving behind a lovely hand poured cement pad. Sure, it's ugly, but at least it will give me more room for a BBQ and chairs, and there's power out there for lights and music and naked orgies. Anyway...

My project today is body disposal. I have to get rid of all this rotting wood, and I'm too poor to hire anyone to haul it off. Carter suggested cutting the wood up into pieces, stuffing it in bags and putting it in the trash. That sounds like a fine idea. I figure after filling one bag with cut wood each and every week it will only take about four or five months to dispose of the entire rat condo. I never said Carter was a rocket scientist.

My trashcan is small, and I have to use it for my regular household trash as well. I dismiss Carters' idea as too much work and stupid. For the past six months, I have devoted myself to the major endeavors of sitting around feeling sorry for myself, not

9

showering, watching transvestite prostitutes fight on the Jerry Springer show, and putting off the task of sawing wood. Well, only because I have no sawhorses.

You see, I have a power saw, but I have nothing to balance the wood on. I'm a practical gal, and the thought of accidentally sawing off body parts really doesn't appeal to me. A trip to the ER, especially since I have no medical insurance, doesn't appeal to me either. Then it hits me. The previous owner left behind these two wooden benches, and I could use them as sawhorses. There are times when my brilliance surprises even myself. So, I make a grilled cheese sandwich, crack open a cold Newcastle and set up the improvised sawhorses. This plan just couldn't be going better. I grab a piece of wood, walk over to grab the saw and stop dead in my tracks. A huge spider the size of a hubcap is living on it. Umm, wow, this is creepy and icky and I scream like a four-year-old girl. Then I remember I am supposed to be a sophisticated woman who can saw wood and drink a beer, while being "fierce" at the same time.

I scream again and back away from the saw. I start making excuses for myself about why I can't engage in hand-to-hand combat with the spider, "Did you see the size of that spider? I think a small child was riding it like a pony! I don't know where I put the directions for the saw. I can't remember how to operate the saw."

The excuses continue in a steady stream through my brain. Now my phone is ringing, and it's almost time for Jerry Springer. The topic today is, "I Slept with Your Sister and Your Mother" so I make a hasty retreat. The saw is still out there. So is the spider.

I am a moron.

SPLASH POO MANSION

Home ownership is a challenge, especially when you lose your job. Don't get me wrong; owning a home is also a great deal of fun. Here's an example – I can paint the walls any color I want. I don't have to ask anyone's permission, I can just paint, paint like the wind!

I have learned it's better to be in a positive frame of mind before the painting begins. After I was laid off, I was a little upset. Fine, upset doesn't quite cover it. I was a crying mess, so I decided to paint the dining room Ralph Lauren Red. I figured a stylish dark red dining room would perk me right up. My neighbor Ken had a fit.

Let me tell you a little about Ken. Ken has the best looking house in the neighborhood. It's a gorgeous two-story Craftsman, painted seven colors which blend perfectly into three basic shades. Ken is the coolest guy in Oakland. Really. He is the unofficial Mayor of our street. Whether he's mediating disputes between screaming women, comforting people in trouble or parallel parking my car when I just can't do it, this man does it all. He's a jazz musician, a perfectionist and it's his voice I hear ringing in my head just now saying, "Girl, don't you paint that wall red! Wait until I get over there."

I don't wait. I paint one strip by the doorframe. Did you know, that if you want a red wall, you have to prime in grey first? I didn't either. Do you know what you get even after three coats of red if you don't prime correctly? You get pink. I know. Lame. I should have listened to Ken's voice in my head. I left that strip of wall pink for five months just to remind myself that sometimes you need to slow down and listen once and a while.

Yes, the house has its challenges. Like the fact that the old lady who sold me the house, may she rot in Hell, neglected to tell me the living room roof leaked. She knew about it, because she had the huge stain on the ceiling painted over. I know this because once the roof started leaking, the huge brown stain that had obviously been there for quite some time started to show through the new paint. That roof must have been leaking for three years at least. Did she mention it? No. She just painted over the stain and pretended like nothing was wrong. Not only is this immoral but it's illegal. That old bat is lucky I just wanted a solid roof and didn't hire an attorney to sue her.

You might wonder if that's the worst there is or if perhaps I found rats eating the wires? No, what I have discovered is worse than rats, much worse. It's Splash Poo Mansion and it's right next door. In fact, our two houses are so close together I could lean out of my bedroom window and touch my neighbor's house, not that I would want to.

What is so horrible about this house? It's a pit. A dirty, dreary pit, smelling of despair and desperate neglect. The windows are thick with grease and cobwebs shroud ledges, dead plants and small animals. It's a third world country without the machine gun toting thugs, wild animals and lack of food. What does it have? Cats. Lots of cats. I'm talking about ten cats in a 1,000 square foot house. Now if it was just the cats, that would be one thing, but it's worse. There is trash piled all over the house, on the furniture, on the floor. The local dump has nothing on this house.

But wait, there's more! My bedroom window looks into their dining/living room, and what do you think I see? A dining table? A couch? No. There is a twin size mattress pushed under the dining room window, and it's covered in cat feces. Yup, you heard it, a mattress full of poo.

Now, cats are clean animals. If this mattress is covered with poo, I can guarantee you there is poo everywhere in that house because those cats don't have a clean place to go. Let me say that again, a mattress full of poo!

Why the name Splash Poo Mansion? Well, I am a huge fan of Disney and go to Disneyland often, as do my friends. One of them told me they were in the Park, behind New Orleans Square on a busy day and heard an interesting thing. In an effort to direct traffic to popular rides, a cast member got up on a low wall and started yelling, "Splash!" "Pooh!" "Mansion!" while gesturing in the direction of Splash Mountain, Winnie the Pooh and the Haunted Mansion. My friend thought that Splash Poo Mansion sounded like my neighbor's place and the name stuck; a little like the poo that's all over their house.

I just couldn't believe this hot mess of a house. I would show this train wreck to anyone who came over to visit: friends, relatives, the cable guy. Please, step this way and view this wonderful mattress full of poo! I started taking pictures of peoples' reactions when they realized what they were seeing. I thought it might make a good coffee table book. I even had an idea for the title, "Poo: The Many Faces of Horror." I know, I really need to get a life.

I just couldn't understand how someone could allow this to happen. It was disgusting. Civilized people shouldn't live like this. I can understand if you're in the slums of Calcutta and have no choice but this? I called the Oakland Health Department and reported the residents. What happened? Well, you will be glad to know, the City of Oakland supports your right to live in a third world country. They told me the only way they could take action was if there were rats, elderly persons on the property or infants. Well, no self-respecting rat would live there and the two residents were middle aged so I was out of luck.

My friends tried to get me to face the facts of what was going on right outside my bedroom window. During my housewarming party, I received some great ideas, which became more elaborate as the night wore on and the alcohol consumption increased. My friend Paul suggested I go over there, knock on the door, speak in an accent, tell them I'm their neighbor from Uzbekistan, and that in my country it's customary for the newcomer to give a gift to each of their next door neighbors. I would then present them with some curtains and offer to hang them for them. I dismissed this as impractical. I mean honestly, where would I find curtains at this hour?

Paul kept after me with this plan. He was like a terrier after a rat which seemed very apropos, "Go on, go over there, I'll go with you." The booze was making this sound like a good idea, but my common sense took over. I had no idea what I would even say. No problem! Paul has the answer for everything, "If you don't, I'll go over there myself, knock on the door, point into the room and just say 'Mattress full of poo?' I mean really!" This idea was also dismissed as unworkable. The bottom line was I had to live next to these people and they knew where I slept. Literally.

It seems the great number of onlookers, attracted by the mattress full of poo, was drawing the attention of my less than clean neighbors. It's hard to ignore crowds of people peering into your dining room with slack jawed horror. Around midnight, Mr. Splash Poo tossed a white lace tablecloth over the empty curtain rod above the mattress, partially blocking the room from view. Well at least something was going right!

Deprived of their carnival side show fun, my party guests staggered home, driven by their responsible designated drivers, and I fell into an exhausted slumber, trying not to think of the pile of poo so close to my sleeping form.

I have a really bad feeling about this.

THE RISE AND FALL OF WESTERN CIVILIIZATION OR WHY THE DOT COM BUST SUCKS ASS

After a two-week "vacation," I figured the spider would have vacated the saw. I went back outside, in search of some fresh air, exercise and spider redemption. The spider had departed for destinations unknown, but I still couldn't bring myself to cut any more rotten planks. Let's be honest, sawing wood is just too much like real work, and exercise is bad for my mental health. So, in lieu of productive wood chopping, I decided to do something truly shocking. I decided I was in desperate need of a mint julep and a power nap. Hey! Being unemployed is a bitch, don't judge me.

Here is my typical day:

6am: Get up, figure I should do something productive like look for a job or send resumes into the Ninth Ring of Hell called the internet mailbox. Turn on the PC, stare at the screen then go back to bed.

8am: Get up again. Turn on the TV; watch TiVo of previous night's "America's Next Top Model." Marvel at why the pretty girl gets booted for being 142 pounds and 5'8" and the bitch on wheels who needs to eat a sandwich gets to stay. Wonder why I can get the flu and not lose weight. Still weigh more than booted model wannabe. Really want a grilled cheese sandwich. Go back to bed.

8:30am: Get up for good. Look at my e-mail, think about looking at Craig's List for jobs, but remember all those resumes that went into the black hole of cyberspace Hell never to be heard from again. Get depressed and look at dancing hamsters on the computer instead.

9am: Turn on TV for background noise. Put an organic blueberry waffle in the toaster. Figure it's better than eating candy. Not like I have candy.

10am: Start looking for Jerry Springer on my new best friend – the television. JERRY! JERRY! JERRY!

11am: Really nice and sunny out. Wonder if purple flannel PJs can double as a tracksuit? Decide that fashion guru Tim Gunn would bitch slap me for even contemplating this.

11:30am: Decide to take a shower but am put off by the fact that my shower has no water pressure (another thing I failed to check before home purchase). It also runs out of hot water pretty quickly. Decide to suck it up, shower and get dressed.

12pm: Go outside and do some gardening. Pull a few handfuls of clover. Steer clear of the black widow condo (the stacks of wood and bricks). The spiders are out to get me. Get winded. Enough cardio for one day. Go back inside to make myself a gin & tonic with extra lime.

12:10pm: Get pulled into watching various cartoons depicting the lives of the unemployed on the Internet. Wonder how these guys find all this time to make little comic strips and movies. Look around and realize if I was half as ambitious perhaps Yahoo would be making me an offer to buy my website. Start drinking.

2pm: Call all the friends I can think of who are also on the public dole or at least have strange job hours. Ramble incoherently about bear dogs or something else incomprehensible. I don't even make sense to myself anymore. Perhaps it's the gin?

2:30pm: Contemplate leaving the house but everything I can think of costs money. Movies cost money, shopping costs money, driving costs money, bars - money, walking – too dangerous and tiring, Starbucks – money, food – money. Decide there is a reason the TV is my new best friend. He's a cheap date.

3pm: Turn on Law & Order because I can never get enough of Briscoe. Did you know you can watch about ten episodes a day on TNT? It's true.

4pm: Decide to put tape on the cat's paws and watch him levitate while trying to get the tape off. Now that's good for hours of fun right there.

5pm: Decide I need a game plan for tomorrow that includes sending out resumes and talking to recruiters and .. Who am I kidding?

Feh.

MOLD, RAIN AND POORLY DRESSED MEN

While still searching for a job and cleaning the house, I have made a discovery of horrific proportions. What could it possibly be? A dead mouse? A nest of cockroaches? Sigourney Weaver's ass?

No, it was worse, and believe me there are few things in the world scarier than Sigourney Weaver's ass in the movie <u>Alien</u>; her white granny panties splashed across a screen two stories tall.

It was mold and not just any mold. I think this mold was of alien origin, due to the fact that I have never seen any mold quite like this. It had to be from outer space. I've heard about those aliens who have been snatching Billy Bob Rubeck and his relatives down in Squirrel Butt, Arkansas and giving them anal probes. I'm sure if Billy Bob could figure out how to work a computer, he would be telling everyone that would listen (the National Enquirer) and everyone that could care less (the rest of us) about how this mold came directly from those gray aliens with the big heads you always see on the cover of various gossip rags. I'm convinced this is part of their nefarious plan for world domination.

You see, I discovered Chauncy's food bowl has mold underneath it. MOLD. Technically the mold was growing on the napkin I put under the bowl, but it was a clean napkin and the bowl was only there for five days. The mold was super long and hairy like some hippie chick's muff or something. I'm talking some major mold here.

I tried to deal with this in a logical and adult manner. I went nuts. It totally squicked me out. I don't do mold, so I tossed the cloth napkin in the bin because I am so not washing that. It might be a sentient being that will want to kill me in my sleep. The cat just looked at me with amber eyes devoid of pity. I glared back at the cat, since this is all his fault. In my mind he is in league with the aliens and had something to do with growing this five-day mold. He is completely nonplused.

I busy myself with changing his food bowls, making sure to check for alien hitchhikers along the way. The kitchen is chilly and it's raining today, so there goes my "water the garden" project. I have no idea when the onions will be finished growing. Hey farmers! How do you figure out when the stuff underneath the ground is done? There are no pop-up thermometers. Farmers are smart. My cat is smart. He secretly grew mold. I am jobless, husbandless and have been infiltrated by aliens from outer space, so I am not so smart.

Which brings me to the state of men nowadays. I started wondering where all the "good ones" have gone and why some women get so freaky after they finally get married and have a kid. One of my girlfriends told me one of these freaky women cornered her at a party and asked her if she was married with children. When my friend told this social x-ray no, the moron actually got in her face and hissed, "Your life is cold and empty!"

What the hell? I think the best response to that comment would have been, "Well I'm sorry you feel like that, but obviously you're so unhappy being tied down when I am free to spend time with as many men as I want and take off to Monte Carlo at a moment's notice. Yes, my life is so very empty."

As for the men, whatever happened with dressing like a gentleman? A rogue, but a gentleman, like Rhett Butler, something snazzy. Every time I turn around I see "men" with their pants down around their knees. Here is a news flash for you guys, this is not cool, it's ugly. I thought it would go away eventually like the tube top or a bad dream, but apparently I haven't woken up yet.

What most of you guys don't understand is this look started in jail. Yes, as in prison. It marked you as someone's property. Guys, jailhouse fashion is not fashion. Unless you really are some skinhead guy's bitch, PULL UP YOUR PANTS. Thank you.

Actually, since I am dishing out advice, here is a little golden bit - no one wants to hear about how good you are in bed. Why? Because if you have to talk about it all the time, guess what? You're no good in bed. If you were good, you wouldn't need to talk about it because all the girls you slept with would talk to each other and the word would get around. If you have one of those "mustache ride" shirts – burn it! It does not get you laid, it gets you laughed at.

I have decided that if the pool of men is this shallow and filled with heinous dressers, I'll pick the cat.

KILLER CLOWN FLU FROM OUTER SPACE

I have no idea how I got sick. I realize there are viruses and germs and all kinds of nasty little buggers that people pass around like a bong at a college frat party, but since I am unemployed, I don't go out. Scratch that, I rarely go out. I'm not Howard Hughes. I don't lock myself in a room and piss in bottles, but I don't have a great deal of contact with the unwashed masses. I guess one of the masses was Typhoid Mary because I now have Killer Clown Flu. What is Killer Clown Flu? I can't believe you have never heard of it.

Killer Clown Flu is the nasty virus that makes your head swell to twice its size, fluid pour out of your nose, your eyeballs dry up and you feel like there's a very hefty midget sitting on your chest. Wait, that isn't a midget, it's my twenty pound cat perched on my chest like a looming vulture of doom. Fine, you can ignore the chest symptoms unless you want to count the hacking, phlegm filled party that has parked itself there.

I discovered another down side of not having a husband is being alone while you hack up a lung; no one is there to fetch or carry or care, except the cat. He is currently looking at me in a discerning way that proves he's just figuring out what bits of me would be best to eat once I snuff it.

Fortunately, my good friend Ruthie came by with some aloe Kleenex, so I could stop blowing my nose on my shirt, and a tasteful gift bag filled with over the counter pharmaceuticals. I was so grateful I could have sworn she was wearing some kind of

Florence Nightingale outfit and was surrounded by a nimbus of radiant light. Then the Nyquil kicked in and I passed out.

While it's bad enough not to have someone bring you grilled cheese sandwiches and tomato soup in bed, the fall-back position for the single gal is the pet, usually a cat. If you're unlucky, even one cat will give you the title of "Crazy Cat Lady." I personally think you first need a fleet of felines, in addition to flyaway hair and horrid fashion sense, in order to be a real Crazy Cat Lady. I also never understood why this only applied to cats. You never hear someone called a "Crazy Dog Lady." Nope. It's always the cats, and they usually come in groups in order to qualify. Since I only have one, I'm not ready for Crazy Cat Lady status. However, being a pet owner has its downs as well as its ups and this is all the more apparent when you're ill.

Honestly, all I want to do, aside from having the aforementioned soup and sandwich, is lie in bed and wheeze. It seems the cat has other plans. He bounds onto the bed like the devil himself was chasing him. Then I see something on the sheets... Gee? What is that? Is it mud? No. It's not mud. NO! It's poo. Great. It seems the cat acquired a hitchhiker from the cat box to my bed. Hanging from his back leg hair was a moist poo clump that clung on for dear life and would not drop off. It freaked the cat out, so he tore around the house trying to dislodge the intruder. It was my luck that it came off on my bed in a smear. I'm sick and now I have to strip the bed, change the sheets, clean the cat and crawl back in bed.

Does the cat care that I'm at death's door and have to clean up his poo mess? Nope, not in the slightest. All he's concerned with is that a piece of poo adhered itself to his ass and would not let go. In my cat's world, this is all my fault. I somehow made this happen. He is equally unperturbed that I have to make a trip to the Laundromat so I can wash the poo stained sheets. I really don't want them to hang around giving off such a lovely odor. This means I have to get dressed and drag my clown head out of the house. I really hate having to go out when I'm sick; especially when it's cold and wet out. A house servant would really help here.

My voice has passed sultry, passed croak and ventured into the "I am losing my voice to cigars and gin" realm. I just don't talk. I stumble to the Laundromat, wash my sheets and try hard not to look at anyone. It would not do to scare the children. I wonder how I go about getting a human house servant who would work for kibble or Cheetos? I know, it's a lost cause but it's nice to think about.

At least a human would be able wipe their own ass.

THE GRUMPY CALIFORNIA COW

Have you ever had one of those days when you set your finger on fire and have no idea how you did it? No? Well being sleep deprived as of late, I managed that feat with very little conscious thought. You see, I've been having a spot of neighbor trouble and not the neighbors from Splash Poo Mansion. They are pretty quiet considering. I'm talking about my new neighbor on the other side of my house. I'll call her "The Grumpy Cow".

I woke up at 5:20 this morning. It's still dark and I have only recently recovered from my horrible bout of clown flu. I need to do some contract work on the PC. So there I am in my dining room, in the pitch black, with only faint light coming from my bedroom because my neighbor, The Cow, complains when I turn my dining room lights on. She says it's like the sun is blazing into her bedroom. She wants me to get curtains. I want her to get a sleep mask.

How did this start? Well about a week ago there is a knock on my door and a very well fed Mid-Western farm girl with a penchant for wearing 1980's fashions two sizes too small is standing on my stoop glaring at me. I just look at her. Honestly, she rang my doorbell so it's her obligation to start the conversation. It's not like I read minds...much. So she starts with a sigh that denotes the task is onerous and obvious at the same time. I just stare.

"You need to get curtains."

I consider this strange request coming from a complete stranger. "Excuse me? Who are you?"

"I'm your neighbor. I live next door. Your dining room light is so bright it's like the sun blazing into my bedroom."

"Excuse me?" I am a bit taken aback. Who is this person and what the hell is she talking about?

"It's way too bright."

I take a breath and try to sort this out for the crazy woman looming over me. "My house is ½ a story taller than your window line and my dining room overlooks your living room. Your bedroom is in the back." (I know this because I was in her flat when it was owned by super cool people and their cat. They moved and made me and Chauncy sad.)

"Well it does."

I try not to point out the huge hole in her argument. Obviously she was not sleeping in the living room and would not get any direct light from my dining room. I only have five 80 watt bulbs for Christ sake. "Why don't you hang curtains? If it bothers you, you can get those heavy black out curtains that are lined."

"I have them. It doesn't work. The light in your backyard shines right into my bedroom window as well."

"That's a security light and I am not turning it off. It's down by the basement steps and doesn't shine directly into your window."

"It's too bright. If you don't turn them off, I'll contact the owner."

Now we have hit the fun part! Here is my opportunity to take her out in one blow. "Ummm, well you just did that. I am the owner."

"Oh." She seems a bit confused by that. However she recovers quickly and barrels on. "The light is still too bright."

"Have you tried a sleep mask?" I ask with a note of genuine concern that I don't feel.

"Yes, the light still comes in."

"You realize that the string part goes in back and not in front?"

She gapes like a carp. I shut the door in her face. Her audience is over.

So, now in order to avoid World War III, when I get up at 5:30am to work on my computer, I leave the dining room dark and work from the guttering light of a single candle. Okay, it's the ambient light from the bedroom but for all the good it does, it should be a guttering candle. Same thing.

The commercials are wrong. Not all California cows are happy cows. This one is a grumpy cow. A very grumpy cow with horrid fashion sense. But enough talk of the light war with the not-so-happy cow next door, I know you really are dying to know how I set my finger on fire. Well, I'll tell you, I was trying to light a stick of sealing wax (which isn't wax at all but some evil plastic substance that passes itself off as sealing wax) while using matches that burn really fast in the plastic stuff. Why was I doing this? I was sealing thank you notes and had to get them in the mail. I have to multi task in order to get anything done these days.

So, I am finishing the last one when I smell something funny and realize that one of my fingers is on fire. Okay, it was actually the acrylic tip of my fingernail but this yellow/blue flame was flickering merrily away. I just stare at it before my sleep deprived brain kicked in to exclaim, "IT'S ON FIRE! PUT IT OUT!" Jolted back to reality, I blew out my finger like a candle on a demented birthday cake.

Now I have a black spot on my nail tip. Great. I could run into a rich charming gentleman who wants to marry me, but then change his mind when he saw the black soot spot on my fingernail. That about sums up my love life to date, fearing that Rhett Butler will finally sweep into my life, take one arched brow look at me and pass; all due to faulty attention to nail appearance.

I am so hosed.

WOULD YOU LIKE TO RIDE IN MY
BEAUTIFUL BALLOON?

My mortgage payments are killing me. I know, anyone who doesn't live in California, New York, or the Washington, DC metropolitan area just doesn't get it. I bought my house for $330,000. The house is 795 square feet. 1 bedroom, 1 bath. There is a semi-finished basement, but it is a few feet shy of being legal height and is not up to code for human habitation, so I can't rent it. Since the house only has one bedroom, I can't get a roommate. I realize that $330k would buy a huge house on an acre of land in most parts of the country, but here in the Bay Area, this is actually a good deal, or it was at the time.

The average 4 bedroom, 2.5 bath, two story house in my area was selling for $700k in a decent neighborhood. The rest of the nation can start mocking us now, but we didn't know any better. This has been the way things have been for most of my life. I envy people who have huge homes for a fraction of the cost, but then I don't want to live in the middle of nowhere. No offense to all the lovely people who live in Fargo or Waco or Squirrel Butt; I just have no interest in setting down roots there. This is my home, and I know why the cost is so high. I remember the old realtor adage, "location, location, location!" It has never been truer than in the San Francisco Bay Area. If you want to live by the Golden Gate, you pay through the nose.

My mortgage is $1,600 a month, but I pay my property taxes separately so that's another $4,500 a year. This was fine when I had the great job at AOL. I could pay that no problem. Sure, things would be a little tight but not unmanageable. Well, now I don't have a job so this is tight. I'm talking "fat man in a little coat" tight, to borrow a phrase from Chris Farley.

I only had three month's severance pay and the temp jobs I've been working have cut my income in half. So in an effort to keep myself afloat I decided to re-fi the house. I know I haven't had it a year, but I only had my job for three weeks before I was laid off. I went to talk to some of the brokers (snake oil salesmen/carnival barkers/creepy banker mimes) and we discussed a flexible, sliding rate mortgage for five years with a balloon payment.

What is that? Hell if I know, they made it sound like puppies and kittens on Christmas. Basically, my mortgage would be reduced to $1,000 a month. It would go up $100 each year and then at the end of 5 years, I would owe a balloon payment of $45,000. The reason behind doing this is simple. It bought me time. I could pull money out of the house, use that to pay off the bills I had racked up with the new roof and repairs, then turn around and sell it before the balloon payment was due. The 45k would just be wrapped up in the sale price. Sure, I wouldn't make a huge profit like that old lady, may she rot in Hell, who sold me the house, but perhaps enough to get by for a bit until I found another job. It was a great plan.

So, thanks to financial smoke and mirrors, I paid off my debt. Credit cards, Home Depot, my car, are all paid off now. Technically I am "debt free." I realize I owe more on the house, but I pay less per month until I can put the house on the market and sell it. It's a perfect plan. It's a great deal! What could possibly go wrong?

Well, home prices started to waver. People started to think, "Hey, maybe I shouldn't be paying $750,000 for a falling down piece of crap in a gang infested neighborhood! Am I smoking crack?" Prices are still decent in the large cities, but buyers are starting to get scared. They don't want to buy something that is going to be worth half the price in a few years. Just so you understand, Californians have been hearing this for years upon years. The old refrain of "the market can't take these prices" or "the market will have to correct itself" has been ignored just like the boy who cried wolf. Housing prices kept going up and up and up. Prices would level out from time to time, but the bottom never dropped out of the market.

Buyers were leery. They were looking but not buying. They were waiting. I thought I could just wait, the whole thing would blow over in a year or so, I could sell the house and everything would go back to normal.

Normal has never been the same.

DURIAN – THE BANE OF SOUTHWEST ASIA

So today after spending an hour pouring over alien re-fi papers, which are as incomprehensible as my original mortgage papers, I needed a break. I mean there is only so much legal terminology you can look at before the whole document starts melting in front of your eyes like a bad 60's acid trip. In order to save my crumbling sanity I turned to my best friend. That's right, the TV, and decided to watch the Food Channel. It reminds me of things I don't have (like food) and some things I've eaten in the past that I wish I could forget.

Allow me to introduce you to the only thing scarier than an IRS tax attorney: durian. The very sound of the name, not to mention the smell, strikes fear into the hearts of many. If a porcupine decided to mate with The Bog of Infernal Stench, this would be the fruit of their love.

Sexy bald adventure Chef Andrew Zimmern from the Travel Channel's Bizarre Foods, has tried to conquer durian eleven times in his life and just cannot get through it without gagging. The putrid smell, the slimy soft mouth-feel and the taste of "completely rotten, mushy onions" does him in each and every time. The late Anthony Burgess, a British novelist and travel writer, compares eating durian to "eating sweet raspberry blancmange in the lavatory." Anthony Bourdain of No Reservations, while a lover of durian, relates his encounter with the fruit as thus, "Its taste can only be described as...indescribable, something you will either love or despise...Your breath will smell as if you'd been French-kissing your dead grandmother."

This blight on humanity reeks so bad that some hotels, and eating establishments across Southeast Asia have banned the prickly fruit within common areas both inside and outside. "Don't smoke, light incendiary devices or eat durian within 50 ft of this doorway." I heard of its reputation and then got an opportunity to try it myself.

Foreign food markets are a cornucopia of possibilities and durian can be found, though in a chemically sprayed form, in certain large cities. If your city has a thriving Asian community and a market that imports fruits you don't recognize, chances are they will have durian. I bought one of the demon fruit and they cut it open for me with a box cutter.

First clue: Any fruit that needs a box cutter, long knife or machete to get past the razor sharp thorns is a problem. I think it's nature's way of saying, "STOP! Don't eat this!" But I'm a moron and I'm willing to try.

The smell. Ummm, yeah. It's the Bog of Infernal Stench. It's like rotting barnyard fun, stinky French cheese and Lurch's feet after a three-day bender in Saigon with some local fermented jungle juice, a pig and a pile of compost. Yeah.

I thought I could be wrong. Andrew Zimmern could be wrong. I mean there are some things that taste better than they smell. Um, no, not in this case. I fought that urge to gag and cry at the same time. The custard gone bad feel of the fruit combined with the taste of rotten onions and an undercurrent of the High School boys' jock straps after a football game was overpowering. How do I know about the locker room? Don't ask. It involves rodents.

Anyway, it was a nightmare. If you really hate someone, get them to eat this. I can't believe that some unknown company in Southeast Asia actually makes a Yule log flavored with this abomination and sells it on the internet. Well, to each his own.

I'll stick to my deep fried shrimp heads thank-you-very-much!.

HOW NOT TO GET LAID OR MISTAKES YOU SHOULD NEVER MAKE ON A DATE

Now that I've returned to the homestead with a brand new mortgage, some money in my pocket and breathing room, I've turned my attention to my love life. In my life I've had one fantastic, amazing date, a few good dates and a whole lot of forgettable ones. In fact, I found a poem on an old card the other day. It's one of those cards that come with flowers. I have no idea who wrote it nor do I really care. I figured if I cared for this guy at all, I would have remembered. Since I didn't, I chalked this up to one of the forgettable dates.

While I realize I said yes to these excursions and continued to see some of these guys, I also realize you need to kiss a whole lot of frogs before you give up, kill them all and have frog legs for dinner with a lovely Chardonnay.

To be fair, I thought I could help some other gals if I school the men on what not to do. Guys - here is the bottom line. If you want to get laid, don't do these things on a date. It's just that simple. These are compiled from my extensive library of dating disasters.

1) <u>Don't try too hard.</u> Women like confidence. If you try too hard, you look desperate. Desperation isn't attractive and will never get you laid. Doormats are for wiping your feet on. Don't be one.

2) <u>Don't babble</u>. In fact, conversation is its own chapter. Conversations should be a give and take, with each party given the

opportunity to talk, but if you want to get laid, give her the floor if she wants it. Don't be a hog.

3) <u>Know when not to talk</u>. Guys, this is the most important thing you will ever learn. Pay attention. If you want to get laid, LISTEN. Don't talk, LISTEN. Even if she is talking about her cat, even if you are bored out of your skull. If you want to get laid, listen - smile - nod appreciatively - let her talk. Look interested. Ask a few questions about what she is talking about but never bogart the conversation. If you are a great listener and seem genuinely interested in what she is saying, you will greatly increase your chances of getting laid.

4) <u>Don't argue</u>. There is a thin line between discussing an issue and arguing with the lady. If you want to get laid, agree with her. Don't argue. It just makes you look like a douche.

5) <u>Don't brag</u>. We like confident men but not braggarts. If you have to brag about your car, boat, job, money, the tip, money, family connections, money, etc., we see you as an insecure git. I once had a mafia bagman (yeah, a real one) take me to a fancy French restaurant in a chic area of LA. He had the chef open the kitchen just for us, bragged about his money, his car and his job in "Construction/Waste Management." He also bragged about how much of a tip he left. Then he asked if I wanted to watch "Das Boot" in German back at his place. yeah... right...

Needless to say, I turned down that offer as well as future dates, even with the offers of fur coats, jewels and a condo. Nope. I do have standards. Guys, all your dough won't make you cool. If you're a wanker, you can't buy class.

6) <u>Pay attention to personal appearance/hygiene</u>. You will not get laid if you have bad breath, dirty clothes or you smell. If the dog tries to bury you, shower and change your clothes. You don't have to be decked out to the nines but be put together and clean. A nice appearance says, "I care about myself and you." If you sweat a great deal - put on double antiperspirant because pit stains will not get you laid either. By the way, make sure your pants are covering

your ass and your underwear. That pants on the ground style is annoying.

7) <u>Be on time</u>. There is no such thing as fashionably late. You are just late and that is bad. If you are going to be late, call. Being prompt says, "I respect you and your time." Being late says, "I am a self-centered jerk that doesn't give a hamster fart about you or your feelings."

8) <u>Don't talk about other girls you've banged</u>. It's in bad taste, especially if your date knows them. If she loathes the girl in question, the whole evening slides downhill from there. Now she is picturing the two of you and guess what? Three doesn't fit in that picture, especially if she loathes the girl. You get written off right then and there, for bad taste if nothing else. Bzzz thanks for playing but you can pack your knives and go.

9) <u>Don't be cheap</u>. This doesn't mean you need to spend tons of dough, but Burger King or cold cereal or some hole in the wall, God forsaken, roach infested eatery from a country no one can pronounce is not appropriate for a date. Don't whine about how $14.95 is too expensive for an entree. Guess what? It isn't. If you can't afford it, be creative. Girls appreciate creative. How about a picnic? That is always cool. Get assorted cheeses, Carr's table wafers, a bottle of wine and some olives. Perfect. A bowl of Captain Crunch? No. Never. Ever. Not if you want to get laid. Guess what? She isn't eight (and the next guy who makes a crack about little girls gets it right in the nards because women don't find that funny either).

To be fair, any chick who orders the lobster on a first date needs to be kicked to the curb. See? Here is a little bit of advice specifically for the ladies. Ladies - men are not a walking penis with a wallet. Be respectful; don't bankrupt them at dinner unless they did something heinous like sleep with your sister. If they did, take them to the cleaners.

10) <u>Don't bring up religion</u>. Not unless you know your religions are compatible. Why? There is a reason the main cause of human

beings killing each other since the beginning of time has been religion. People get pissy, possessive or just plain fanatical. Remember, you want to get laid. This goes back to #4 Don't Argue. If you don't already have common ground, avoid that ground. That ground is quicksand. Run, Forrest, Run!

So there you go. You should make sure you take notes, and if you aren't a total douche, you should be able to get laid. Have fun responsibly but remember, if you act like an ass, she is entitled to boot you in the junk.

Just sayin'.

THE DREADED CAMEL TOE

I think after that bit of levity, we need to be serious for a moment. Society has a terrible problem and it's going to take all of our best efforts to eradicate it from the planet. War? Famine? Donald Trump's Hair? All child's play. What I am speaking of is ... camel toe.

I try not to think of camel toe too much, and by ignoring it I feel I am adding to the problem. I need to speak out, to raise camel toe awareness. Ladies, why do you feel the need to wear clothing so tight that it's jammed up your peesh like that? Why? Do you think it's sexy? Men, do you think it's sexy? I think on the whole women know damn good and well when they are wearing a camel toe generating outfit and do it because they are attention whores. Any excuse for a man staring at their beaver is just fine and dandy with them.

This is just as bad as men with their swingin' Johnson's jumping ship. Men don't get camel toe but there are those "lucky few" who are so endowed that Uncle Milty has invited them to join his private club. They just let their equipment swing free and if they are wearing short shorts (remember those silky Dolphin shorts?) or sitting with their legs akimbo, BANG! You have a "Free Willy" moment.

This happened to me and it was traumatic. I was on a shuttle going from the Ontario Airport terminal to the rental car place to pick up my cost conscious, compact automobile. Well here I am, minding my own business and I look across the way and there it is, staring at me! What did I do? Well, I gave it 2.5 seconds of intense thought then turned to the gentleman and whispered in the dulcet ladylike way I have, "Dude! Put the mouse back in the house! I mean, I could be a virgin or something!" The guy had the decency to be suitably embarrassed, fix himself and not spread his legs again.

The camel toe rant? Oh yeah, that's what I was talking about. Where did I get my zeal from? Today I had a traumatic experience at Starbucks. It was early, around 6:35am. I'm sitting down with my chai tea latte and there, right in front of me was... camel toe. This was not just any camel toe. It wasn't Beyonce camel toe. It was big, it was scary and it was in my face. I turned and there it was... in my petite flower face!

It was totally traumatic. I lost at least a year off my life. Please help stamp out camel toe. Check yourself before you leave the house, check your friends. Friends don't let friends walk around with camel toe.

Remember, working together we can eradicate camel toe in our lifetime.

THONGS – AN ODE TO EVIL UNDERWEAR

Throughout history, we have dealt with the oddities of strange under garments. Those wacky pieces of clothing, large or small, designed to cover our nether regions for modesty (nuns) or practicality (something to strap your nards down when you are running through the bush hunting wild boar). Underpants have been pretty (La Perla), practical (Joe Boxers), peculiar (a little gourd that covers your...nut) and torture devices (chastity belts). Now in modern times women have a new arch-enemy - The Thong.

As kids, we lived in fear of the dreaded "wedgie." What sense does it make to construct underwear that actually is supposed to wedge itself in the crack of your ass? I fail to see the upside. I can just picture the men all raising their hands and saying "We see the upside!" Yeah, but you don't have to wear it, and if you do wear thongs, you aren't looking at me. Ladies, straight men don't wear thongs and if they do, you don't want to know them. Run. Run like the wind!

Now all your girlfriends will tell you, "Thongs are so comfortable! You just forget you're wearing them." They are lying. They are lying through their teeth just like they lie about how 8" fuck me pumps are comfortable. They're not. Misery loves company and they just want more sisters to feel the pain with them. I am convinced that thongs were designed by men. Not just men - masochistic drag queens. I am sure of it. There is a plot. I'm positive it was cooked up in some fabulous bistro in West Hollywood over Cosmos and conversations about wig styles and who was that trashy bitch over at Hamburger Mary's who thought she could actually work it in those pumps?

I admit I fell into the trap, bought the BS and tried all kinds of thongs. I have tried lacy thongs (too scratchy), tiny thongs (my ass ate them), cotton thongs (too wide and uncomfortable). I have tried them all. You know the one thing they have in common? At some point, you find yourself looking for a corner so you can try to be sly about pulling your thong out of your ass. Ladies, no one is that sly.

Now, just because women have to suffer with the bad panty dance, it seems only fair that men shoulder some of the underwear burden as well. I'm sure there are men out there who also suffer from wedgie complex. In the interest of science, I performed a quick survey of men I either knew by aquaintence or who I ambushed on the street. All of them assured me that underwear comfort was the last thing on their collective minds and that I might want to seek professional help.

Despite the fact that the men declined to participate in my panty psychosis, I think in the interest of sexual fairness, I must needs the question, "Where do men stash their junk?" and give some air time to the male underpants dilemma.

I have to admit, male genitalia mystifies me. I think a great many women would agree with me if they really thought about it. I mean, we don't have any dangly bits. We grew up being all neat and tidy; a place for everything and everything in its place. All our parts tucked up and in and away from view. It's almost like a Martha Stewart Living spread during the Spring holidays.

Men? Everything is just out there. Swinging free, out in the open, letting it all hang out. I am perplexed. Doesn't it get in the way? How do you walk? Don't you catch yourself when you run? Do you chafe? I find the whole concept of going about your daily chores, having to haul your dinosauric penis out of the way every ten seconds, a bit odd.

I also have a theory, that as men age, their testicles fall prey to gravity much the same way as natural female breasts. I have seen 70 and 80 year old men walking around like their balls have descended to knee level and they are trying to knock them out of the way. Is that true? I conducted a scientific survey (consisting of asking three guys, one of whom was my Dad who told me to get off the phone and send out more resumes) and concluded men don't think much about it or plain don't care.

I guess it's just that men, due to their hanging apparatus, appear to have more underwear and/or swimsuit options than women. I thought it was only fair to examine those options. For the sake of decorum and the fact that I have no husband, I will examine men's swimwear (which is close enough to underwear to count).

1) Board Shorts: AKA Jams, my personal favorite. They fit a wide variety of body types and still look stylish. Guys look cool in board shorts. Does it cloak your junk? Sure does. Ladies like to leave something to the imagination. We don't like it in our face (at least if you haven't bought us dinner first); as you will soon see.

2) Boy Shorts: These are the abbreviated Jams. More like Daisy Dukes if the truth be told. Ladies look hot in them. Men only look good in these if they are gay with hard bodies and on the strand at Palm Beach or Boca Raton.

3) Bikini/Speedos: These are a classic look but you need to be careful. These are for athletes only. If you're Michael Phelps, they're hot. If you're Ron Jeremy, they're scary. They also seem to go better with the sleek, hairless or spare hair variety of body. Papa Bears just look uncomfortable in a Speedo, like they lost a bet or something. Remember Ben Stiller in "Meet the Parents?" Enough said.

4) The dreaded Banana Hammock. This is the male thong and it is more evil than any thong that girls wear. Why? Think about it. Remember how I said that ladies don't want your junk thrust in their petite flower faces? The banana hammock is the worst offender. What makes things even more heinous, these travesties

of fashion are usually worn by fat men from the Jersey Shore. Yup, lots of hair, gold chains, and a large belly overhanging their package that is strapped into a rubber band device of medieval design. It's not a pretty picture. I really don't even want to see Antonio Banderas in a banana hammock. The truly sad thing is how proud these guys are. "Look at me and my Jimmy! Aren't I cool and studly? You want me, don't you!" Ummm... no. No, we don't.

Another small thing to note: Forget the six-pack. Do you want to know the sexiest part of the male body? It is that cut from the hip bone down towards the leg. Hot.

Let's make a deal, let's just say no to torturous underpants that other people want us to buy. I believe this one small thing will make the world a whole lot brighter.

THE HORROR OF SEE'S CANDY AND WHY I'M PISSED AT BEBE

Over the years, I have funneled hundreds of dollars into the City of Oakland's coffers. Today is street cleaning day. This monthly ritual means that my car needs to be off my side of the street from 9am – noon. When you're working, street sweeping day is never a problem because your car is gone; however, being a member of the "Great Unwashed" (unemployed) means putting money you don't have into the City kitty.

Yes, I was so lazy I forgot to move my car last night and all the spaces on the safe side of the street are taken. I know it's my own fault but all these tickets are starting to get old. I'm sure if they keep accumulating I will have to sell my cat into feline slavery. Sooo, that only means one thing, road trip! I put on some make-up, shrug into some decent clothes and drive to Walnut Creek. I have See's candy to exchange and I know there is one shop at the little open air mall in the downtown area.

You see, my Mom always sends me a box of See's Candy for Valentine's Day. I got mine in the mail two days ago. I open the mailing box and see it's dark chocolate. How many times do I have to say milk chocolate?! Ummm, since I was eight? I will eat the occasional piece of dark chocolate, but I don't like all dark chocolate. I have given up trying to clarify this (I wonder if my sister got the milk chocolates?) so I just figure it's easier to return the box and have them get me a pound box that I pick out.

I get to the store early, and they aren't open yet so I go to Nordies because I need jeans. My friend Christine is threatening to throw mine out because they are so worn. I see the cutest jeans and then I have heart failure - $280. FOR JEANS! (breathe, breathe) I become frustrated that jeans now cost the equivalent of the national debt of a small South Pacific island, and I need something to distract me before my blood pressure gets too high.

I head upstairs to lingerie. If I can't buy jeans then I might as well give the thongs Christine swears are comfy a go. I'm willing to play panty roulette one more time and throw good money after bad on yet another type of thong. I search the rows of lacy book marks but I don't see the miracle thongs anywhere. However, I do see a great many boy shorts. I assure you they are only to be considered underwear in the slimmest interpretation of the word. In fact I have never seen a pair of knickers so narrow.

I tried to take a picture on my camera phone but don't know how to upload it. I need to read the manual. These panties are tiny! I mean, they are narrow, maybe five inches tall at most. I'm trying to figure out how these even qualify as underpants since they're a straight rectangle band that would barely cover the naughty bits of a twelve year old kid. Oh, and they are $35! So after this latest clothes trauma I decided to return to my original mission. I throw in the towel, or the thong if you prefer, and head over to See's Candy.

I arrive twenty minutes after the store opens and it's packed. WTF? Then it hits me...tomorrow is Valentine's Day. Great. Valentines is the worst holiday on the calendar. I am now stuck next to desperate husbands standing in line for candy. Three of them are toting Victoria's Secret bags in a pathetic attempt to get laid.

Okay, guys, let me help you out. No matter what people say, girls don't want candy. You don't want to buy them candy and have to listen to more of, "Do I look fat in this?" You will have your sweetheart blaming you because she dove into that heart shaped box and added ten pounds to her ever spreading ass. Honestly, ditch the candy. I can hear you now, "What about the Victoria's Secret stuff? Girls love Victoria's Secret. Isn't that gift guaranteed to get me laid?" Nope. Their underwear is poorly made, it doesn't fit right and guys never know what size to buy.

Once I was in Victoria's Secret and some guy was trying to pick out a gift for his wife but didn't know her size. He was completely clueless to the fact that various bras of the same size can fit differently. He was pointing to j-random women, all with different sized breasts and swearing she was his wife's size. Maybe he's Mormon and is buying a variety pack.

I went up to him and said, "Okay, close your eyes. Now picture your wife naked. Do her thighs touch or is there air between them? How big are her boobs? Grab them in mid-air." Yeah, I'm a giver. Guys, if you really want your wife to love you for the underwear I have two words. La Perla.

Anyway, after dealing with the candy exchange horror, I decide to go back home when I find myself walking past Bebe. Eureka! There is the cutest shirt in the window. It makes me feel pretty just looking at it. I go in and try on a few things. The sizes are way smaller than they say. The good news? The cute shirt fits and is affordable. The bad news? It has 234,000 tiny hooks on it with the loops near buried so it is impossible to close. I spend ten minutes trying to hook this demon corset top and cursing the gay man who designed it and obviously hates me.

I stomp out of there in frustration telling them that when I was a size 4, I tried on this darling purple coat with purple fur collar (I know it sounds hideous but it was really cute) and the collar was held on by 543,899 tiny hooks. Every time I took the jacket off, the hooks came undone and half the collar flopped off. Why should I pay all that money for clothes I have to have altered?

I hate Bebe and all of the teeny clothes and desperate men and stupid red satin heart boxes of candy and that wanky squirrel who just ran in front of me on my way back to the car. It stopped, sat there and just stared at me. Great. That was a little creepy and unnerving. Little was I to know it was a sign of things to come. I head over to Christine's so I can unburden myself of the angst and tiny underwear trauma and the fact that I have no jeans. Christine has the answer to that. Macys. She swears that is where the "perfect thong" lives.

Maybe tomorrow.

EXTREME HOME MAKEOVER – PAINT AND PREJUDICE

After all the excitement both good and bad, I've been forced to do a bit of reflection. I have decided that as long as I am in this house, I really need to commit to making it my own.

The old lady, may she rot in Hell, painted the rooms a pale yellow and white before she sold the place. It may not seem like much, but it is a far sight better than the dark Kelly green the walls were before she painted, or the sea foam green I found inside cabinets on the back walls. Obviously the painting was the idea of her stager and what a good idea it was. The mental institution green would have driven most people to distraction (or medication) and she never would have sold the house.

Believe me, paint is the easiest part of this nightmare. The kitchen was straight out of the Ninth Ring of Hell. It was tiny, narrow, sported a smelly fridge and an avocado green stove that didn't work. By law, all homes for sale in California must have a working stove. She listed a toaster oven, which was present during the walk-through and would qualify as a cooking appliance under the law. When she moved out she took it. Not that I wanted it, but without it she was breaking the law yet again, may she rot in Hell.

The floor was comprised of peel and stick linoleum tiles from the 1970's. How do I know this? I found a box full of them in the garage. They were brittle with age and the stickum on the back was far less tacky than the design on the front. While it was easy to remove them with a putty knife or the side of your shoe, they still gave me the creeps. The glue stains they left behind on the subfloor, made the wood appear mottled with mold and age. A close inspection showed the wood to be sound but the appearance did nothing to ease my mind.

If the floor fracus wasn't bad enough, the back kitchen window was busted and held together solely by large strips of duct tape. The window set into the back door was busted as well. Yes, this is the house I decided to pay $330,000 for – don't judge me!

So, before I could move in, I needed a new fridge, a new stove, new paint, a new window, a new back door and a new floor. Appliances are the easy part. You just call someone, pay for the appliances you want, they deliver, set up the new ones and cart off the old ones. Easy! No problem. The floor was a bigger challenge. Why? Because it had to be finished before the new appliances could go in. This required bribing various people to move the old fridge and stove into the dining room, rip out the nasty stick-on tiles and replace the entire thing with Pergo wood.

I've never been much for power tools; although I have watched the DIY Network and Extreme Home Makeover a lot. Ty Pennington makes it look so easy. I didn't have Ty Pennington on speed dial though. I have friends I can call for these kinds of situations, but not a hot handyman with rippling muscles. The kind of handyman you can only imagine shirtless on the cover of novels that use words like throbbing, hard and turgid. Whew... is it getting hot in here? Nope, I love my friends but they are not ripped and turgid or ripped, turgid and single (which is what's important).

So once the floor was down, the new appliances installed and the old ones hauled away, it was time for... painting! I didn't want to make the same Ralph Lauren Red mistake I made when I was first laid off, so I went to ask my neighbor Ken. In addition to being called the Mayor of Vernon Street, I also call Ken the Paint Nazi after The Soup Nazi from Seinfeld. Although Ken would never shout, "No paint for you!", he has been known to put you in time out for poor paint prep and color choices. Don't get me wrong, Ken's happy to lend a hand and pass along the fruits of his labors.

So why the nickname? It's because Ken is hard core when it comes to paint.

Did you know that painting involves more than just slapping paint on a wall with a brush? It's true. The prep is more than half the job. First, you have to empty the room. Then, you cover the floor with brown paper that you need to tape down, and next, you sand the walls. You heard me, you sand the walls. My walls are plaster so the sanding smoothes out all the bumps. Now you mask all of your edges with that blue painter's tape. After that, you must prime your walls before you paint. Let me tell you, I'm tired just typing that. Can you imagine doing it? It's a lot of work, but Ken knows his paint. He has the best-looking house on the street and is not afraid to tell you what colors work, what colors don't and how to achieve that great looking result. It isn't quick, but it's right. Yup, do it this way or, "No paint for you!"

We both agree the best thing to do is to choose colors that complement the architecture. I know some people may love bright purple or Pepto-Bismol pink but keep it off your house. It's just nasty. Since my house is in the Craftsman style, I picked some warm colors. I decide on a deep golden yellow, a terra cotta, a sage green and a dusty peach for the various rooms. The kitchen's makeover, with its deep yellow and peach accents and copper hardware, transformed that space from a depressing, sterile, cubbyhole to a warm and welcoming area, even if it is the size of an airplane galley.

I had also ordered a beautiful door with a Craftsman style stain glass inset. I was preparing to stain the door with a deep redwood gel when Ken came sauntering across the street.

"You better be masking off all that brass hardware Miss. If you are out of the blue painters tape, just holler and I'll get you some of mine. Oh, and don't forget to tape off the rubber as well because the stain will get on it and break it down." I dutifully did as he directed, he nodded and walked back across the street. Ken knows everything.

What does Ken do for a living? I think he's a retired jazz musician. There are nights when I have the front windows open and hear the most amazing music coming from across the street. It's lovely and haunting. If I close my eyes, I can picture myself back in the French Quarter in New Orleans. It's magic.

JOB INSANITY

In the old days, when you were looking for work, you would go to actual stores and ask for applications, or you would look through the want ads in a newspaper and make phone calls. Now you use the Internet. Craigslist has become the modern day equivalent of newspaper want ads for job postings. I hate our Brave New World. Why? You send your resume out to an email address and there it goes, whoosh, into the Black Hole of Hell, never to be heard from again.

Applying for jobs also takes longer than ever before. Some large companies want you to answer a page of questions in addition to what you've put in your cover letter, but the government is the worst. They usually want you to fill out a ten page application which includes a whole passel of essay questions. It can take a minimum of three hours or more to fill out, just for one position.

Now, I know there are millions of people looking for work and they are all competing for the ten good jobs that seem to be out there. This is prime time for employers because they can make people jump through more hoops than a God damn circus poodle. In fact, they can even request that applicants dress like circus poodles. Don't believe me? Well, I found this job on craigslist. It's for an admin to a C level executive. He appears to run a solar energy company.

To apply, you must submit the following. These materials are mandatory, and your application will not be considered without them.

51

• Compose a short cover letter that discusses your passion of solar energy, compost and recycling.
• Write an "elevator pitch" about what sets you apart from other candidates.
• Prepare three PowerPoint presentations on:

(1) The future of solar energy in Canada and the Ukraine. Compare the two.
(2) Standards of recycling and the way they can be improved in a green forward manner.
(3) Your personal story, or your proudest moment, as it relates to the Solar/Green movement.

Ummm, are you kidding me? The job isn't for a C-level executive that will be running a division, it is for an administrative assistant. You know, a secretary. This is the person who types your letters, keeps your calendar and drops off the mail. I thought perhaps this was a bizarre screening device. If someone was actually nuts enough to do this and make it look good, it would weed out 99% of the idiots who just apply to every single job on craigslist regardless of experience.

Now, if something like that, for a "normal" job, takes a couple hours, government jobs are even harder. First, you have to fill out never ending applications on-line, and if you are deemed worthy, they are followed up with an hour long test at some local government institution. Before the economic bust, scoring in the upper 1/3 was good enough for an interview. Now? Not so much. If you don't score over 90% correct, then forget it. You are a loser, but don't worry, you can apply again in three months. How do I know? Because I'm one of the losers. I scored 82% correct on their arbitrary test and I failed.

This makes me think, why should I even bother? Even with the leading multiple choice trick questions, these jobs have awesome benefits including pensions. It is also harder to be laid off from these jobs. Job security is a good thing. This just leaves one nagging question – how did some of these mental midgets that I've dealt with get these government jobs in the first place? Perhaps when they took the test, the bar was set really low. Maybe just doing the job sucks the smart right out of you. That actually makes sense, but it doesn't stop me from trying to get into one of these coveted positions.

I guess I'm just a whore like that.

GYMS – THE AGONY OF DEFEAT

You would think being out of work would give me plenty of free time to exercise, lose weight and get in shape. I wish. One of the downsides of unemployment is fighting the ever-present feeling that nothing is ever going to be right again. It makes you want to crawl in a hole and pull the dirt over you like a demented mole. Okay, a mole with beer and a fuzzy gummy worm I found in the bottom of my purse.

I decided to go on the South Beach diet. Carbs are my enemy and it's a healthy way to lose weight. The hardest part of this eating plan is Phase 1. This entails two weeks of hell where you can't have any carbs. So, no fruit, no corn, no carrots, restricted dairy and no booze. I can deal with meat and veggies for two weeks but no booze? Come on! I know a diet is great, but you have to follow that up with exercise. That's my big problem. I don't run unless someone is chasing me, and a glass of wine or a frosty Tiki drink are great motivators.

I started thinking about why I don't exercise more. I figured it was just too much work. Gyms make me really uncomfortable. It's almost like they hate me. I realize they serve a useful purpose. They do. They also cost money that I don't have and serve as temples to narcissism. They were the 80's answer to pick up bars.

Allow me to illustrate the various types of gyms I have seen:

Upscale Celebrity Gym: LA is flooded with these. Thanks to reality television, we even get to see the inside of one in particular.

Jackie Warner's Sky Sport has been featured on the show Work Out, where we get to see cat fights, lesbian affairs and high priced bods in all their glittery glory. Personally I would feel like a huge cow next to the Mr. Universe/WWF guys and gals that frequent a place like that. I would feel dumpy, ugly and so not fashionable. That would be the worst part. Not to mention the fact that the price tag would kill me.

Corporate Gym: Now this is one gym I do know. I loved the gym on the AOL campus. True, it was a way to escape my low-pressure shower but I also got addicted. This is the secret of gyms. The chemicals your body produces from working out cause an addiction just like sugar or chips or a Mint Julep on a hot day. I would get up at 5am, drive from Oakland to Mountain View, get to the gym at 6am, work out, shower, get presentable, and be at my desk at 7am. I would even do this when I was flying home from a weekend in sunny Southern California for months on end. I would get home at midnight, but I still needed to be up at 5am so I could hit the gym. Yeah, I was addicted.

I used the weight machines mostly, the bike (because I could read while I pedaled) and the elliptical because it was fun. No one bugged you, you didn't have to lock your locker and I could team up with my co-workers Also, since I was there so early in the morning, seeing other people was rare. That is always a plus in my book.

Pick Up Gym: These gyms, like Gold's, are gyms you joined a week after New Years in a flurry of guilt and self-hatred. You were lured by their "New Year's Special," dazzled by their juice bar, still hated yourself and never returned OR you went and got hit on by guys whose thighs were the size of tree trunks. Sure, they can crack a Brazil nut with their butt cheeks but their IQ is about as high as my bust size. Their conversation skills are about as exciting as watching snails race. One of my girlfriends summed it up best, "Unless you look like Brad Pitt, don't talk to me. Don't bother me with your lame excuse for conversation. I'm here to sweat, not to get hit on."

Chick Gym: We've seen these mysterious buildings, usually down an alley or in a strip mall; floor to ceiling windows covered in pink pleated curtains. Yup, it's the "women only" work out place. I imagine these gyms are free from judgment, comfortable and the curtains serve to keep gawkers to a minimum. This is in direct contrast to the pick up gym, since gawking is part of the experience there.

I mean, honestly, why do you think celebs and gym rat people spend so much bank on work-out clothes? I could wear sweats, nasty tennis shoes and no make-up to Curves. To Sky Sport? Not so much. I would need new outfits, shoes, make-up, hair and liposuction so I would look cute when I glow which still means don't talk to me unless you are Roman Coppola.

I remember the old chick gyms as a child. I would watch women sitting on those rotating drums with the bumps on them or the famous vibrating belt machine. How anyone thought shaking your fat around like a giant jell-o dessert on ground zero of a Nevada proving ground would actually work is beyond me. Perhaps some sick bastards thought it was funny. I guess this is why they put the curtains up. The last thing women need is the judgement.

Neighborhood Gym: When I was a junior in High School – Go Trojans! – my dad was a member of the Quail Lakes Racquetball Club. Racquetball was big back then. It's a fast game and I liked it. Okay, I liked the little shorts and carrying around the racquet. I was 100 pounds soaking wet and after hitting the ball into a wall on an enclosed court for fifteen minutes I decided it was too hard and I was more into hanging out at the juice bar. I can't play racquetball now. It makes my boobs hurt. I didn't have boobs then. I can prove it. I have a plaster model of my naked torso an artist friend of mine did in 1992. I had A cup boobs. It's in my basement, you can see it. What does this have to do with the racquetball club? Nothing, except that it's harder to exercise when you are not a twenty something ninny that needs to eat a sandwich.

So, those are my observations. Pick the one you like or discard them, but I warn you, there is truth in all of them. Just sayin'.

Me? I'll just go back to my deprived of alcohol, Phase 1 South Beach diet existence and dream of rum.

WHY COLDSTONE CREAMERY FREAKS ME OUT

I just finished a week at a temp job. Yay! Go me! Any money is good money and actually earning a little extra made me think things were starting to turn around. At least I had extra dough to buy myself a treat. Treats come in all shapes, sizes and monetary levels but I think we can all agree that ice cream is a fine treat. I've wanted to try this new ice cream place called Coldstone Creamery ever since their advertising wove its way into my dreams.

There's a phrase, "A picture's worth a thousand words," and it is especially true when I think of Coldstone Creamery. What do I mean by that? It's simple. The pictures you see on the website make their ice cream creations look like some beautiful, mouth watering, ice cream wet dream. They drive me crazy just looking at them. What's wrong with this? Nothing except it's a LIE. A lie I tell you! Am I smoking crack and mainlining jelly donuts at the same time? No, nothing like that. Besides, I don't like jelly donuts, they woog me out. Why all the hating on Coldstone? Allow me to explain.

A few years back Coldstone Creamery was coming to the Bay Area. There were billboards off every major freeway featuring pictures that tempted me with promises of orgasmic ice cream glory. I dreamed about this ice cream. I imagined what these various flavors would taste like, and one day a Coldstone store finally opened in Emeryville.

I practically ran into the store. I was so excited to be able to finally taste these creations I had only seen from afar. The pictures all over the walls just affirmed this was where I was supposed to be. I was in Heaven. I ordered one. I believe it had apple and caramel and pecan pieces in it. This bored kid behind the counter put the items on a frozen sheet of metal and started mixing the ingredients together with these paddles and do you know what happened?

The lie happened! What ended up in my bowl did not look like the beautiful picture with all the items easily identifiable. What it looked like was a red hot mess. It reminded me of when I was eight years old and I threw stuff into a bowl of ice cream and stirred it up until it was a smooth, unidentifiable soft serve puddle. Guess what? I'm not eight anymore. Here is another news flash: nothing they make looks like any picture they take of it ever!

To make things even worse, the moron behind the counter held me captive and made me listen to some dork ass song they had to sing. I was told by Coldstone experts they only sing the song if you tip them. Ummm, after the mess I was presented with, would I ever tip anyone? I thought perhaps my experience was not usual or it was just this guy or this store but NO. Even my friend Gerald agreed that the mixed up mess of ice cream destruction was a disappointment.

To me, ice cream should remind you of your childhood, like Baskin Robbins, or take you to a place of nostalgia coupled with handmade quality you don't find anymore like Fenton's or Lourd's. Ice cream can be funky and socially responsible like Ben & Jerry's or decadent and elegant like Godiva or Robin Rose. But it should never be mediocre. Ice cream is too important to be treated like the shell game in a cheap confectionary carnival.

I REALLY HATE YOU COLDSTONE CREAMERY. You are the Devil. Especially since I've been carrying around this $5 gift certificate, and now I am conflicted as to what to do with it.

SEDONA PISSES ME OFF

Today, all of my phone-in temp job leads have fallen flat. Determined not to make a total waste of my day, I decided to walk to Whole Foods and use their free wi-fi to send more resumes into the Black Hole of Hell. While sitting there in my corner, minding my own business, I was forced to listen to two crunchy vegan chicks, eat their gluten free, vegan muffins and regale each other in loud voices about the wonders that are Sedona, Arizona.

This takes me back, and not to a happy place. Sedona stands out in my mind as a source of bitter disappointment. It just makes me angry and pissed off. Well that's not entirely true. In order to explain this newest affront to my delicate sensibilities, we need to go back in time... (Insert time travel sound effects of your choice here)

Okay, a decade or so back, my BFF Roxy and I were going on a road trip. We were housemates, and her mother lived in Arizona at the time, so it was off to Phoenix for us. I figured, since we were trekking all the way to Arizona (in Roxy's red jeep that rattled), that we should make a side trip to Sedona. Roxy didn't want to go. The conversation went something like this.

"Hey, when we go to Arizona, I want to go to Sedona, it sounds so cool."
"You really don't want to go there."
"Yes, I do."
"No, you don't." She gave me that special earnest look. You know the one mothers give to their kids when they want to eat all

their Halloween candy in one go. That earnest look says you'll be barfing Skittles by bedtime but there is no way to get that through your thick skull.

"Yes, I really do. It sounds so peaceful and amazing, I have to see it. "

"Trust me on this, don't go."

But, I persevered, she gave in, and we went. I was totally one of those candy eating kids and even the threat of projectile vomiting couldn't stop me. I wish I had listened to her.

Sedona is the wart on the Devil's left tit. Why? Have you seen Sedona? It's not like the postcards. It's Hell. Yuppie Hell. Crystal swinging, tantric chanting, freaky Atlantis reincarnated alien Hell. It's a bad acid trip in turquoise.

First, let's start with the architecture (if you can call it that). It's a faux Southwestern nightmare. Everything seems to display a bandana wearin' coyote abomination. Everything is coral and turquoise. Even the Golden Arches on Mickey D's are fuckin' TURQUOISE. That is just wrong.

Second, you can't swing a dead squirrel without hitting some crystal channeling, past life regressing, hippie freak of nature spouting Atlantian "wisdom" and alien abduction theories, which they will gladly impart to you for the price of an SUV. I was always told that the difference between the Craft and New Age is the decimal point. That's a fact. These idiots are fleecing people for big bucks. P.T. Barnum was right. There's a sucker born every minute.

Third, the "residential family communities" people are clambering to get into are abominations. The wonderful, serene beauty of the red rock bluffs is now home to private, expensive gated compounds where people can "commune" in private; walled off from the rest of the planet they claim to love. If I were a Native American I would be pissed. In fact, I would not stop a whole hoard of Native American spirits from riding through the town on their horses and killing everyone in sight.

What has been done to this sacred land is a travesty. It's unnatural. These people are unnatural. If you are sooo into the peaceful beauty and spiritualism of the area, why exploit it? Why turn it into a freaky New Age sideshow? These so called gurus go on and on about how spiritual they are. These people have no clue. I hope in their next life, they come back as squirrels.

That said, I had to feel a little sorry for the clueless vegan chicks. If they really think the city of Sedona is the pinnacle of beauty, they obviously have never seen Yellowstone or Yosemite or even the Sequoia National Forest.

Then again, they think vegan muffins and donuts are tasty.

THE SHED OF DOOM

The metal shed from Hell, which occupies most of my backyard, is fast becoming the bane of my existence. It's about fifteen feet long by ten feet wide and comes equipped with its own electric hookup that accommodates heavy-duty three prong plugs. It seems to me that the former owner's husband did a great deal of work out there. At least enough to warrant getting the underground electrical installed.

Currently it houses paint, gardening supplies, tools and the body of said old lady's husband. You remember her? The one who is currently vacationing in the Bahamas on my money, after selling me a house with an illegal roof that leaked and a non-functioning stove. Alright, maybe his actual body isn't there, but I am half expecting to find it under the basement sub-floor or in a wall or something. Why?

Neighbors talk. I'm telling you, there's something strange going on. When I bought the house, I was told by the neighbors that Mrs. X's husband died three years before she sold the house. What was the cause of death? I haven't a clue. Heart attack, Alzheimer's, sheer desire to get away from the Missus? Could be none or all of the above. Now, I have uncovered a few things that have given me pause.

The first thing is the toilet. No, not the toilet in the bathroom, the toilet in the garage. Yes you heard me right, a working toilet wedged between the water heater (again, installed illegally as I found out later) and the washer/dryer (which never worked, but she generously threw it in implying that it did work). The second odd thing I noticed were all the outlets in the basement. There are tons of them, all along the wall at shelf height. There is also a working sink and a dead bolt on the main door that works from the inside but has no external key. My conclusion, the old man was hiding out from the old lady, spending all his time in the basement watching TV and growing massive amounts of pot.

The shed also seemed to be part of the old man's grand get away scheme with the heavy-duty electrical outlet and all this storage space. Well, now it blocks my view, takes up 2/3 of the backyard, and I will never be able to get rid of it. I found out it's not possible to take it down myself; even if I do get a better ladder, climb on the roof, and brave the spiders. I would so fall through the roof and kill myself. This would be bad, especially if I landed on the tools.

I would need a minimum of two people, and that's not happening. This only leaves me the option of trying to find non-rapist males who are bonded (so, less likely to kill you), pay them to take the shed down and then pay for a bin to dump it in. I weigh the options of living with the rat condo or sucking it up and making a call to get some men over to remove it. Paying the men won out, especially since they recycle. It almost made me feel like a socially responsible Berkeley hippie.

I called and made an appointment for this week. They are going to bring a huge bin, cut the thing apart and then haul it off to be recycled. Pity they can't remove the black widow condo while they are at it. Currently it's covered in weeds, which I have to remove next week. The spider killing outfit of choice will be long pants, long sleeve shirt, and thick leather gloves with a heavy duty whacking stick. I figure I have to man up at some point and get past this spider fear or at least learn how to deal with them. This is part of the responsibilities of home ownership. I may be single and plagued by psychotic rodents but I can do this!

Honestly, who needs a man when you have a whacking stick?

WHAT WOULD I BAN

Now, a bagel on a Sunday may be a lovely thing, but it pales in comparison to the multitude of food choices out there. I adore food: good food, comfort food, exquisite gourmet food. Yes, I am a self-proclaimed foodie and make no apologies for it. I believe that fresh, non-processed food is one of the greatest gifts we have been given and one of the best things we can do is to share that bounty with those we love. I started thinking about what I would ban from eating establishments if the country, or the planet for that matter, ever decided to vote me Queen Bitch of Everything.

<u>Guilt:</u> Guilt at ordering water from the tap instead of a bottle or instead of a soda or a beer. If I just want water that I could go into the loo and get from the sink for free, why make me feel bad? Double for "Doggie Bags." We all know the dog isn't getting this. It's my food. I paid for it so I'm taking it. Ditto for the wine and yes you can take it with you. Cork it, bag it and put it in your trunk. No problem. When I used to wait tables, I would feel bad for people who asked for a box with that apologetic note in their voice. I told them, you paid for it, of course you can take it! That also goes for the bread. Take that too. They are just going to chuck it in the bin when you leave and it's a sin to waste.

<u>Dirty, Crusty Condiments</u>: This especially applies to ketchup bottles. Someone hasn't been doing their side work correctly. Report that. Yes, they do refill the bottles from other bottles but the caps should be cleaned and the necks wiped off.

<u>Ground Pepper</u>: Perhaps in the 70's it was all posh to have the waiter grind and grind over your plate for a dusting of black pepper. Sorry but this is lame. If you are eating fine food and you have a decent chef, your food should never need extra seasoning. However for other establishments, there is pepper on the table. USE IT. It's not like peppercorns are truffles that must be doled out in careful portions and with great ceremony. This is as dated and lame as huge white plates in weird shapes.

<u>Pretentious Poncey Waiters</u>: Okay, your job is to serve me, not for me to be dazzled by your fake accent, your pronunciation of Viogner or Tilapia. Don't treat me like something you have to tolerate, unless I give you reason to earn your distain (then you can touch my food – I've done that before to obnoxious customers). Anyway... be helpful, don't hover and don't show off. Be efficient but not an insufferable know-it-all.

Here's a true story. I was waiting on a young couple. It was a first date or some type of "I want to impress her" of celebration. He had brought a bottle of sparkling wine with him. I opened it at the table and... wow... it had a plastic cork. I could see his face fall a little. I did a bit of David Copperfield, palmed the plastic stopper into my apron and replaced it on the table with a real sparkling wine cork. He was grateful and my tip reflected that.

That is your job, now DO IT.

THE SQUIRREL FROM HELL

While jobs have been few and far between, I did find one great upside to living in this house. Spring. More specifically, the beautiful flowering tulip tree in my backyard. Actually it's in my neighbor's backyard but it's so immense that some of its branches hang into my yard. But wait. Don't let all that beauty distract you. Be warned. Amongst the green leaves and pink tulip flowers, high in that tree lives the most fiendish creature ever to wear fur - the Squirrel from Hell.

Why is he so evil? I don't know. Why did Ming the Merciless oppress the planet Mongo? This furry fiend from Hades taunts me. Now before you think I'm a big pussy, let me explain something. This is not a simple taunting. This is a sophisticated campaign of terror conducted at the highest level. It's a thought out mind game on the caliber of high-level intelligence organizations such as the KGB, the CIA or Disneyland.

Now, I admit that I inadvertently started it. I was trying to be nice to the woodland critters. I ignored all rules of common sense and left chunky peanut butter on the fence. It turns out that Skippy chunky is the equivalent of squirrel crack and this guy wanted more. So, I started scattering shelled peanuts on the ugly cement slab where the shed used to be. He buried them in my backyard. I thought that was fun and entertaining. That is, until he grew bold and started bringing the peanuts up on my deck, sitting on the rail and hurling them at my kitchen window, all the while chittering madly like some furry demented fiend.

What the FUCK? Was he pissed that there wasn't peanut butter on the fence anymore? Did he not like the peanut shells? Did he want my soul? This was starting to freak me out.

I'll admit I don't possess much in the way of wee rodent knowledge. When I was little, I thought squirrels were the ambassadors of fun. They would scamper, caper and cavort. They were cute, fluffy and well dressed. Now I realize they are really rats with better fashion sense, Cthulu in a mink coat.

The other day while I was puttering around in the backyard, because that's all I am capable of doing in the yard, putter, I heard a noise that sounded an awful lot like a herd of raccoons. It was coming from somewhere above my head. It wasn't raccoons. Raccoons would have been quieter. Plus, they're nocturnal. It was the squirrel, scampering along the fence ledge. He stopped, chittered at me, then launched himself into the tulip tree, onto the shed next door, and finally into my lemon tree, where he plucked a wee deformed lemon off a branch and lobbed it at my head. FUCKER.

My shotgun was too far away, so I grabbed the hoe and charged him. He just leapt back into the tree and off he went, screaming like an Ebola ridden gibbon monkey. I just stood there looking stupid.

Squirrel - 2   Me – 0

SHOPPING HELL OR DOES THIS MAKE MY BOOBS LOOK GINORMOUS?

After getting my ass handed to me by a demonic rodent, I needed to get out of the house. I decide to get motivated and go clothes shopping at Anthropologie. I need clothes for job interviews, they are having a sale and I came home with four things. I should be happy, right? Well, you would be wrong. Here is my nasty secret. I didn't try anything on. I relied on the sizes printed on the labels of my cute, on-sale clothes and got a nasty surprise.

First, I found this one really cute vest in what I thought was my size. I somehow neglected to allow for the fact that my boobs have grown over the last decade from an A cup to a D cup. I was thinking I was a small C cup when I went shopping. I was mistaken. I can button the vest if I don't breathe, the result being that my boobs look ginormous. I know, you are thinking that I am an idiot to be complaining about ginormous boobs when women pay $5,000 - $8,000 for fake ginormous boobs. I realize that, but the flip side is that this ginormous boob look will kill me. Because I can't breathe. So, I'll be dead and no one will want me except some creepy necrophiliac.

So anyway, there is a cute dress I saw in the catalog and I've been coveting it for months. I found it on the rack, it's in my size and it's on sale. Score, right? It was $40 off (go me!) and it was in the same size as another dress I have from Anthropologie, but this has a side zipper and my waist is just 2mm too big. Now I have to suck it in as much as I can and bend myself into a pretzel to get the thing closed. And pray. Praying is always good to head off a possible wardrobe malfunction.

Guys, you should know that women are all freaked out about clothes because while the sizes say 2, 4, 6, 8, 10, etc., that doesn't mean that all 8's are an 8. That 8 could really be a 12, labeled an 8 to make gals feel better, or a 4 to make them feel like a T-Rex. Designers are evil hags. The size manipulation just adds to our sense of self-loathing. This is why I don't try things on in the store. It's that sense of defeat and humiliation that I hate.

Oh, did I mention the pants? No? Oh, that was because shopping for pants in the sale area was like shopping for Nicole Ritchie or some other stick who needs to eat a sandwich. Let's see - sizes 0, 2 and 4. I don't think I can get a thigh into the waist of those.

The frustrating thing is I used to be a stick girl. Yup, I have size 0, 2 and 4 dresses. All those XS vests and size 4 jeans. I need a fuckin' donut now. I was way too skinny. I had people thinking I was barfing up my dinner when in actuality I had the metabolism of a crazed weasel. What happened? Did I face plant into a tub of ice cream. Actually, no. It seems that once I hit thirty-five, some demented fairy (helped along by birth control pills) came along and decided it was time for my woman body. Say bye bye to those size 4 Bebe dresses. I will never wear them again.

This just makes finding nice pants for job interviews a journey through the Ninth Ring of Hell. You see, this is why I don't shop. It's just too depressing. What I really need is a job where I don't have to wear clothes. Ummm, scratch that. That would be totally icky and weird unless it was a society of nudists on a South Sea island. Fine, I will stop digging the hole of justification deeper. I really just want a real job so I can focus on more important things. Things like world peace, a green society of sustainable energy and making a bigger trap to catch the evil squirrel.

Now that would make me happy.

JESUS LOVES ME THIS I KNOW

I haven't had much luck in the dating department. I will own the fact that I'm really picky, set in my ways and have picked some psychotic idiots from the bin of bad ideas. I like to think I have improved on the idiot ladder but they have never really come close to my idea of the perfect man. Who would that be? Well, think Rhett Butler, Fitzwilliam Darcy or Captain Malcom Reynolds. Sure, they are all fictional characters and I have an ice cube's chance in hell of any real man living up to that, except possibly for Alan Rickman.

So in order to make sure I have a man who is strong, kind, fun, a little freaky and totally perfect, I have decided to marry Jesus. Yup, THAT Jesus. It's not such a strange thing. Millions of nuns the world over are "Brides of Christ." I decided I would be a regular wife instead of just an old spinster with a pipe dream and really ugly underwear.

Where did we meet? Well it was kind of a funny story. I was on this secret mission for the Norwegian government that involved some rare art, a Welsh Corgi and a herring. Fine. I was at my local Starbucks, sipping a non-fat, no water, chai tea latte and looking for a job when this hippie guy sat next to me. At first I thought he was going to get his patchouli stink all over me and try to lecture me on my love of animal products, but I was wrong. He was nice and normal and even bought me a chocolate croissant. He started talking and I said, "Hey, has anyone ever told you that you look like Jesus?" And then he said, "That's because I am."

Yes, I admit, I was a doubting Thomas, or Thomasina, if you will. I thought it would be in bad taste to ask him to turn water into wine, but when did that ever stop me before? Hell no! So, I got a glass of water from the Barista and asked him to prove it. He wanted to know what kind I wanted. Well, I thought a nice Rubicon Estate Cask Cab 2000 would be nice. It received a 91 point rating from Wine Spectator after all. Well, you could've knocked me over with a feather, but he did it! Now who doesn't want a guy like that?

Now, Jesus does come with his own posse, so that was another hurdle I had to clear. I can tell you, Mary Magdalene is totally sweet, completely hot and makes this great grilled lamb dish that is to die for. Judas is actually pretty cool, though he does hog the remote control and talks incessantly about topics no one really cares about, but we smile and nod because we don't want to hurt his feelings.

The more I think about it, the more I think Judas has more in common with the regular guy than most people realize. The hogging of the remote and the pigging of the conversation are just the tip of the iceberg. There is also the smug pontificating on the absolute rightness of his opinion, the living way outside his means and the unasked for advice. He means well, really. He wants to be Helpful Hanna but just has trouble with residual social awkwardness. You would think that nearly 2,000 years of practice would have helped him with that but not so much.

The most frustrating thing about being engaged to the Son of God is the fact that no one believes me. I know there are millions of people waiting for Jesus to return, but they think he's just going to drop from the sky in a ball of light, hurling lightning bolts and magically transporting people up to Rapture Heaven. They refuse to admit he could be having a latte at a coffee shop. I've always said that Christ could return to Earth, show up in front of a ton of people, tell them to knock it off with the killing and the intolerance and the judgmental attitudes and they would just nail him to a board all over again. Such is the human animal. We are so flawed.

All we can do is try not to let the flaws of the human race get us down. Believe me, Jesus has decided trying to save mankind from itself is a lost cause at this point in time. Humans are just not interested in a message of peace and love. They are much more invested in finding better ways to kill and torture each other. So this time around, he's decided just to hang out and enjoy the show. Personally that suits me just fine. I have the coolest fiancé, all the free booze he can make out of tap water and we never run out of food at parties.

It's a Win-Win.

ULTIMATE DEATH MATCH 4: CHAUNCY VS. THE RACCOON

My demonic black basketball of a gay cat, Chauncy, is getting old. I always told him that he wasn't allowed to age or get that greasy old cat fur, but I guess it happens to the best of us. Personally, I hold onto the fact that, in my mind, I will be perpetually thirty-four until the day I die. Why thirty-four? Why not?

Chauncy started out as twenty pounds of cat, but now he's a mere shadow of himself at half that. However, this does not stop him from picking fights in the most unlikely of places. You should know that my cat isn't a bully or even very brave most of the time. He has no idea of his size, former or current, and lets other cats push him around. Let's face facts; my cat is afraid of soap bubbles. Yup, you heard me right – bubbles. If you blow bubbles from a wand, it totally squicks him out. He just runs away from them. I have no idea why. He's a cat. He defies logic.

Well, the other day he decided to redeem himself in the "butch cat club" in the most unlikely of ways. He decided to take on a raccoon. Before you make the mistake of thinking that raccoons are cute little sidekicks, like the one from that Disney movie, think again. Raccoons are mean. They have claws, opposable thumbs and could operate small caliber firearms if they could get the aiming part down. They wear those masks for a reason.

I know because I fed a raccoon a Fig Newton once, and he nearly mugged me for the rest of the package. In fact, he came back and brought friends. There is nothing like camping in a thin nylon tent while a pack of possibly rabid furry bandits prowls around your campsite and snarls. Needless to say, I gave up the Newtons, threw them as far away as I could, and prayed the 'coons wouldn't figure out how to operate the zipper on the tent.

That being said, the other day I saw that a raccoon had decided to camp out on the back porch. It seemed he had discovered the small bowl of cat food and water I left outside for the times when Mr. Man would sun himself on the back deck. I thought that after he ate the food he would move on to greener pastures but nope, he decided to take a page from the squirrel's playbook and make my backyard one of his regular stops. Oh, and he had the gall to toddle out in the late afternoon.

I thought raccoons were nocturnal, and if you saw them during the day it meant they were sick or had rabies. Well, this large fella didn't look sick, in fact, he looked fat and happy, but I wasn't taking any chances. I made a habit of looking around before letting Chauncy out, just in case Mr. Raccoon was there. Then one day I opened the door, and I heard the strangest sound. Chauncy was growling.

You see, Chauncy doesn't growl. In fact, he doesn't even meow properly. It's sounds more like "meh." I just answer to it because I figure he's trying. My friend Susan just looks at me with pity, tells me I'm not encouraging him to "use his words." Ummm, he's a cat. Susan doesn't care. She knows he's playing me. But now, he is full out growling. He is all arched up like a Halloween cat, his tail is all brushy and the fur is standing up on his back. What's going on? Then I see it – the raccoon!

I may be a city girl but I know that a raccoon can easily kill my cat and could also lay a heap of hurt on me. I call to Chauncy to come inside but he's having none of it. He hates this intruder and he goes for him. Hissing and spitting, he takes off after the raccoon. Well, I can't let my geriatric cat get eviscerated. So, I grab the nearest object I can find, a broom, and forge ahead to break up a pissed off pussy/raccoon rumble.

The raccoon is just looking at Chauncy like he has clean lost his little cat mind. He waddles off in a casual sort of way, or at least as casual as he can with a hissing cat stalking him. I really don't want to have to fight a raccoon with a broom. It's not a very good weapon, and I especially don't want to have to get four rabies shots in the stomach if I get bit. Chauncy doesn't care; he just wants the interloper gone. He makes a daring run at the raccoon, the raccoon turns and heads to the fence. As Chauncy launches his ten pound ass into the air, I grab him mid-leap and back away from the startled critter who is looking at me with an expression that just says, "WTF?!"

As soon as the door closes, Chauncy is back to his former lazy, fat assed, barely meowing self. Well, I guess he showed that raccoon. "Don't come around here no more man, or I will fuck you up, or at least I would if my Mom didn't get in the way. You are soo lucky my Mom grabbed me." Yeah, I can just hear that going around his little fuzzy brain.

Now after all that excitement, I need a drink.

GROUNDHOG DAY – AN ODE TO
PUNXSUTAWNEY PHIL

Who is Punxsutawney Phil you say? What? Have you been living in a hole your entire life? He has, but that's beside the point. Punxsutawney Phil is the most famous weather prognosticating rodent in the country, perhaps even the world, though I have heard that Wharton Willie from Canada has been angling for the job for years. But we don't have to worry, it's not like Canada is a real country. Oooo. By the way, North Carolina has its own groundhog named...wait for it...Sir Walter Wally. I shit you not. However, there is only one Punxsutawney Phil: the prognosticating groundhog of Gobbler's Knob, PA. Here was Phil's prediction this year, according to Phil's official website, as read at sunrise from Gobbler's Knob.

"It is said that imitation is the sincerest form of flattery.
Around the country there are many imitators of me.
In Harrisburg there is Gus who appears on TV working for the lottery.
Then all around town,
Cute groundhog statues abound.
Hey all look like me, I found.
Today on the Knob as I'm doing my job,
I don't like this likeness of me.
It's my shadow I see. Six more weeks of mild winter there will be."

Tell me, when did we decide to let a hamster on steroids tell us what the weather is going to be? Does this report of early spring or late winter just apply to Gobbler's Knob, the whole state of

Pennsylvania or the entire country? Some days I wonder what compels people to party all night in ass freezing weather just to watch some tuxedo wearing, Rotary Club members haul the varmint out of its climate controlled log, chitter at it in "Groundhog-ese" and then run to the local fire station to stand on line for a pancake breakfast?

The way I see it, Punxsutawney Phil, or PP for short, is nothing less than an All American Hero. How did I make that leap? Well he represents the values we all hold dear to our greedy little hearts.

His entire world revolves around himself. Phil doesn't work. He doesn't have to. He has at least seven guys that take care of his ever spreading ass year round. He has top notch digs and top drawer chow. Everything is tops, from the top hats his gopher keepers wear, to the top revenue he brings into the city. His only job, and I mean only job, is to stick his head out of his hole and look around to see if he has a shadow or not. Now I find out he doesn't even do THAT. His Top Hatted Bosses decide the weather report a week or so in advance, write it up in a fancy poem and then all Phil does is ... well... just show up.

Of course, he has accomplished some important milestones in his long and illustrious career. Here are a few of the highlights from his official website:

- During Prohibition, Phil threatened to impose sixty weeks of winter on the community if he wasn't allowed a drink.
- Phil traveled to Washington DC in 1986 to meet with President Reagan.
- In 1993, Columbia Pictures released the movie Groundhog Day starring Bill Murray.
- In the years following the release of the movie, record crowds numbering as high as 30,000 have visited Gobbler's Knob in Punxsutawney.

Those are some pretty impressive credentials for a talking rat with a glandular problem. See? He embodies what Americans have been doing for years! Between America's pocket dogs and "My

Gifted Kid is Smarter than your Honor Student" bumper stickers, idiot self-esteem entitlement attitudes and Lindsey Lohan rehab stories, is it any reason why I think this rodent is the perfect American symbol?

In the fall, Phil is the guest of honor at a picnic that culminates with people "trekking to the Knob for Phil's ceremonial sip of Groundhog Punch." This is the secret brew that gives Phil his long life and good looks. Yup, you go gopher! Selfish self-indulgence and rehab! I feel kinda bad that I don't get the weather rodent thing, but at the same time I'm strangely drawn to it all. Perhaps one day I will be amongst the screaming mobs in the icy streets of Gobblers Knob, standing in the darkness of the early morning, wearing a plush rodent on my head, drunk on joy and flasked whiskey, shrieking like a mad woman and praying that my shame doesn't end up on YouTube.

I can only hope.

A THONG I LIKE – YES, HELL IS FREEZING OVER, SHUT UP

Men never seem to have a problem with underwear. They have no problem buying it, having it fit or even caring much about it. I'm not talking about the freaks of nature who think banana hammocks are sexy, but the average Joe just doesn't put much energy into it.

Women care, but we have a much more difficult time finding panties that fit. It's not like you can really try them on in the store. You need to guess on the size based on the current size you wear. The problem, as you know if you've been paying attention, is that designers lie to you about sizes, so the size on the label may be way too small (making you feel like a cow) or way too big (making the cutest lace things look like granny pants).

I have no idea what to do. I need knickers in the worst way but nice, lacy panties are expensive! If you make the wrong decision and pick the wrong panties then you are stuck with overpriced, unusable lacy bookmarks. You can't return used panties; that's just nasty and perhaps illegal. I guess you could sell them to pervs on the Internet but I'm too much of a lady to do that. Really!

So, in a fever of spring cleaning, I decided to go through my panties and toss any that were too small, too old, too embarrassing, or too uncomfortable, and the result was, I was left with five pair. Five pair of underwear. Crap. What if I wanted to jet off to Monte Carlo or Disneyworld for a long week and only have four pair of extra panties for eight days? That is just not acceptable. I know, I know. I don't have a job, so I'm not jetting anywhere, but there is nothing wrong with being prepared. After all, television has taught us that things like this happen all the time. Really!

It just isn't fair that I have no job, no marital prospects, and no underwear. This brings me to my original rant, and it is all Christine's fault. Yes! She was right. I was wrong. There I said it. You see, she told me about Hanky Panky thongs, the original cut, not the low rise. I figured I would take her word and flush another $40 down the rat hole on thongs I'm going to hate and never wear, and they will be all scratchy because they are lace, but I will try them. So I buy two pair, magenta and pink. She tells me to try them for two weeks and I will never know they are there. I tell her, she must realize she is casting herself as Charlie Brown. At the end of the two weeks, she will either be The Hero or The Goat. I was already planning my goat song with a goat dance to go with it. Now, like a goat, I'm eating the sheet music to that dance.

I wore a pair yesterday and ... she was right. I'm in love. I really don't feel them. They don't itch. I'm not hauling them out of my bum all the time. They are wonderful, and while I still say that 98% of the thongs out there are evil, these aren't.

Actually, they are evil because now I have been lured over to the thong side of the fence. All I want to do is to chuck the rest of my knickers in the bin and replace them with Hanky Panky thongs. The only thing standing in my way is the fact that I don't have $200 lying around to buy replacement thongs. I could save up and buy one a month like a thong of the month club. I keep telling myself, I'll get my old life back and get a puppy because happiness is a warm puppy, or so Charles Schultz always told us.

Once that happens I can buy all the thongs I want!

JONESING FOR STARBUCKS

Lately my life has been interesting, to say the least. On the up side, I have a temp job. Yay! It's a dead end, soul sucking, low money temp job working for a construction type store in the credit department, but it's a job. On the down side, I slipped on my front stairs on the way to work and broke my ass. Honestly, I broke my ass. Okay, I cracked my tail bone, but it's still the same thing. Busting my ass just about sums up my life right now. It hurts, it makes everything uncomfortable and even if I did have medical insurance, there isn't a damn thing a doctor could do for me except point, laugh and charge me $220 for the privilege. I actually had plans for the weekend and this is not making me happy. So, before I wallow in total self-pity I decide I deserve a little something special and make a foray to my favorite retreat, Starbucks. I know, I know, they are the devil. Don't judge me.

Starbucks has long since become a cultural phenomenon. You either love them or hate them. There is no middle ground. I must say, that even though I'm not a regular coffee drinker, there are certain things I crave. A grande, non-fat, no water, chai tea latte is my current favorite. Remember you are only an asshole if your order is something like this, "I want an extra hot, venti, non-fat, soy, half cap, half drip, with vanilla and hazelnut, lite whip." People with these long-ass idiot orders are douches of the highest order. Just saying. Try doing that at Peet's coffee. Those hippies will kick you in the ass and toss you out on the sidewalk.

Chai is my drink of choice. However there are always the seasonal libations that worm their way into my head. When

Christmas rolls around it's Eggnog Latte. Stop throwing up in your mouth! It's sooo good. My friend Shannon threatened to stop talking to me because of my passion for them. At the time, he was working at Pasqua Coffee (which was bought out by Starbucks). He said if I came into his Pasqua's he wouldn't even make one for me. Thankfully I really like him, so the threats just fell by the wayside. Remind me to tell you about the 70's hippie Bigfoot soft-core kinda porno he showed Ruthie and me. Shannon has some weird movies.

Anyway - Starbucks now has mocha raspberry lattes and frappucinos. They are the new brand of evilness out to tempt me over to the dark side. "Luke...I am your Father. Drink this venti mocha raspberry low fat latte with whip and raspberry sauce." You know, seeing it written out like that, I guess it is a little douchy, but I just don't care.

I always get lite, if the "lite" is Splenda and not NutraSweet or aspartame or some other rat poison derivative. If no Splenda, then just sugar but I need a little whipped cream with the raspberry sauce so I can mix it in. The lite Frappuchinos don't come with whipped cream normally, although the Starbucks around Livermore asked if I wanted whip while the one in Novato just assumed I didn't. I found that out the hard way when I placed my order then stared at the flat topped cup the snarky barista handed me.

"Um, it's flat."
"Yes."
"It's flat."
"It's lite."
"I know that, but its FLAT. Where's the whipped cream and the sauce? That's the best part."
"The lite ones don't come with it."
"They do in Livermore."

The barista gives me the look that says she could care less what the heifers in the hinterlands of Livermore do, but in svelte Marin

County everyone KNOWS that if you want lite, you don't get whipped cream.

"It's flat. I don't want it flat." (Giving her the look that says, "You just squirt my whipped cream, coffee monkey - don't judge me.")

Starbucks is my guilty secret. I suppose I feel guilty because there are more of them than Peet's. Face it, there are more of them than herpes. You can't swing a dead toad without hitting a Starbucks. I will risk missing my plane just to get a latte before my flight. It's sad really.

Their food is also something that calls to me in times of stress, just like a lover or a really wily crack dealer - the cranberry bliss bars and gingerbread during Christmas. OMYGOD! Soo amazing. Their raspberry loaf right now is pretty yummy as is their low-fat orange dreamsicle loaf. They have new salads that are really good, and their tarragon chicken salad sandwich is to die for! I really have to stop doing this, because now I want to run off to a Starbucks and get a latte. It's all part of their evil plan to take over the world, I'm sure of it.

I wonder if they are recruiting minions?

IRISH CAR BOMBS AND GAY ALE

My former housemate Ruthie always tells me I need to get out more, socialize, have some fun. This translates into, "Hey! You can meet guys if you go outside. Guys usually don't just show up at your door uninvited unless they are up to no good." You have to admit, she has a point. So last night I went out with a couple friends. To make things easier, let's call them Jason and Dave, since those are their names. We decided to go out for some munchies and drinks. Alright, it was mostly drinks. To be perfectly honest, it was a small pub-crawl with some food stuck in as an afterthought. You get the idea.

The evening started sedately enough with a pint of Guinness at a local pub. The evening was new, it was still light out, and my only acts of rebellion thus far were crossing the street without using the cross walk and spurning the sign that specifically told you not to. Eat my shorts Law Dogs! Well, after having a nice chewy breakfast beer and a chat with dreadlocked Jamaican twins, the novelty started to wane. Guinness is nice, as are twins, but I was sure there was something more exiting out there in the wilds of downtown San Jose. Eager to start our adventure in earnest we drove to our next stop - the Tied House.

The Tied House is a microbrewery that makes some lovely ales and also serves great food. I know, you're thinking, "Oooo, a microbrewery! How daring! Did you borrow your Dad's car for this exotic law breaking adventure?" Don't judge us, besides I'm not finished yet. We deemed it responsible to order something to buffer the booze before we continued our evening of debauchery.

85

While pesto garlic fries and micro beer might not be your idea of drunken insanity, keep in mind that two of us are responsible for paying mortgages, two of us have jobs and all of us are past our days of chugging Boone's Farm behind the 7-11 or mooning unsuspecting pedestrians from our cars. As you become more mature and responsible, your taste in liquor goes up and your desire to spend the night in jail goes down. Sorry.

After the Guinness I went with a light, fruity ale; passion fruit to be exact. Fruity is right. Anyone who drinks this beer turns flaming gay - I swear. I even called a few of my gay friends to be sure. They assured me it wouldn't do a damn thing for them but were sure it would work on straight guys. A challenge! I made the guys drink it and lo and behold - they turned gay. It's so true. When I called Dave's wife she assured him she would cure him of his gayness as soon as he returned home. The guys went for something amber or hoppy or "normal" with no trace of strange fruits. Stupid boys. No sense of adventure I tell you!

Well, after the food, it was on to our next local pub. O'Flaherty's Irish Pub to be exact. It was here I discovered the most amazing drink on the planet, an Irish Car Bomb. No, really. It's like one of those shots with the strange names like "Sex on the Beach" or a "Flaming Erection" only this one is larger and involves more steps. Honestly, you have to work for your buzz with this drink.

First grab yourself a shot glass and fill it halfway with Jameson's Irish whiskey and half with Bailey's Irish Cream. Next you fill a pint half way with Guinness. Now here is where the fun starts. Drop the shot glass into the Guinness. Now, chug. Really. Chug. Chug. Chug. You need to chug it before the Bailey's curdles everything.

Wasn't that fun? In five minutes the bomb will go off. This makes us brave. Brave like Kevin Barry or Michael Collins. We chugged two of these a piece and then moved on to downing full-sized Irish Martinis which consist of just the Jameson's and the Bailey's. It's getting late and the next pub awaits. If I had a sober thought in my head, I should have gone to the Ladies Room before I left but the bomb went off in my brain and I was singing Kevin Barry as we staggered out into the night.

We're walking and walking and damn I really have to pee and we're walking. Sooo have to pee now. We're walking and discover the next stop on the pub tour is out of business. Fine, we'll go to Gordon Biersch. Walking, my teeth are floating. I'm starting to count cracks in the sidewalk to take my mind off my near bursting bladder. Why didn't I go before we left the pub? Because I was buzzed and stupid. Well I'm paying for that mistake now aren't I?

We get to Gordon Biersch a little after midnight and it's closed. Great. It's barely past midnight, which is their posted closing time. I ask the bouncer if I can just use the bathroom. We only missed being seated by fifteen minutes and there are a lot of people still eating. He refuses. What a dick. I think he secretly wants me to pee in the bushes. If there were bushes.

We continue walking to another pub that's close to the one we had just left. Did I mention I REALLY HAVE TO PEE? We finally find the pub. I break all land and speed records running to the bathroom. Whoa, I feel better now. I feel like a new person in fact. I now understand the adage of "having to pee like a race horse". I think I lost 4 pounds of water weight after that bathroom trip.

In my haste to get to the bathroom, I failed to notice the "entertainment" this pub was providing. On my stroll back from the loo, I have the time to stop and ogle at leisure. It seems the local dork wads are doing rap on this little stage in the corner. Let me clarify that, I'm talking lame ass white people doing really bad karaoke rap in a pub. We are soo leaving. We drank the gay ale, we have culture now, and this isn't it. I grab the guys and steer them to the door.

By now we are running out of options so we head back to O'Flaherty's for another Irish Car Bomb. Drink count for me thus far: three pints of ale, four Irish Car Bombs and an Irish Martini in a six hour period. I'm done. I kept up with the boys, and now I need to crash. I get home sometime after 2:00am. No, I did not drive. No, I'm not suicidal. So after this eight hour booze tour, what did I get? A date? Nope. A medal? Nope. A grope by a stranger in a dark alley? Ick and nope.

I wake up in the morning and I'm offending the cat and myself. I reek. My skin is exuding the unique odor of garlic, Baileys, and various kinds of grain alcohol. Face it - I smell like ass, and I look like it too. The cat is staring at me with equal parts disgust and annoyance. He gives me a few halfhearted kicks as if he is trying to bury me. "Hey Cat, don't judge me." I give up. Trying to keep up with the boys was a stupid plan. I need another plan, a foolproof plan. What kind? I have no idea. I try to contemplate it in the shower but all I can think about is Irish Car Bombs.

I start humming the tune to Kevin Barry.

WHAT IS IN PEOPLE'S BASKETS – A STUDY IN SCARY

After that night of debauchery, I'm trying to keep my spirits up. You know, not having a job is a very stressful thing. I apply for a few more jobs on-line, had two recruiters call me back, ask for my resume and submit me for jobs that don't pan out. I decide that instead of driving myself crazy wondering why no interviews have materialized, I will work on my resume go through boxes in the garage/basement. I really need to go through those boxes, but every time I go down there I get bit by invisible critters (probably spiders) which I'm slightly allergic to. Fact is, it's just another annoying depressing thing that I would rather avoid.

I want to make Sweet Potato Ravioli with Lemon Sage Butter. I saw the recipe in a magazine and it really sounds good. Do you know the feeling of getting fixated on something so much that the let down of not accomplishing it is just devastating to your spirit and soul? Okay, it wasn't that bad, but I'm unable to make this pasta creation because even Whole Foods doesn't have won ton wrappers and if you think I'm taking my life into my hands by going to Chinatown, you are high. The last time I was there, a little old lady, about eighty years old and barely able to see over the steering wheel, nearly ran me over.

I guess I can try the recipe for Roasted Flank Steak with Olive Oil Herb Rub instead of the won ton raviolis I had my heart set on. I have all the ingredients for that, except the flank steak. So it is time for another Whole Foods run. The only immediate problem is that it's lunch time. Lunch time is not the best time for a Whole

Foods run. Not only is the place packed but also the strange people quotient has gone up. While I do see many odd characters there on occasion, right now it looks like a group of them got together over a soy latte and decided to invade at the same time.

I wonder what these people do in their daily lives that they have the time to hang out at Whole Foods? I envy the people in the little coffee area, sitting there with their Mac laptops writing the Great American novel. Okay, let's be honest, it's more likely a militant manifesto on organic farming, but still I envy them their laptops at the very least. They eat their little cartons of food, sip their coffee and look smug.

I haunt the aisles, looking for meat and the odd Mo Better Bacon Bar from Vosges, I start checking out people's baskets. Not those baskets, I mean the ones in their hands. You know what I mean. One guy has a basket full of linseed oil, lavender soda and salt. Hmm, he's cleaning his furniture with assorted ripped, gay underwear models. I've had that soda. It's good, but straight guys don't buy lavender soda. They are too afraid of it. It's the same with the mini vegetables.

There are two "ladies that lunch" arguing over the merits of Annie's organic bunny pasta vs. some frozen organic baby slop. I feel the need to offer up thanks for being spared their scary lives. "Thank you Jesus for sparing me the life of organic baby slop." I never wanted to be pregnant. I'm way too vain. I think being pregnant is gross and it scares me. My eggs are stale anyway so I really shouldn't worry, but I do. One of my funny friends, Diana K, said it best, "Babies are like puppies that hate you." Truer words were never said. The ladies settle on one of each and run off to squeal at hemp baby clothes. I shudder and the last of my stale eggs just went toes up.

A free-spirited hippie love child runs by me in her cheap polyester nightgown from JC Penny's. I swear! She was wearing brown polyester pants with huge bell bottoms, some clunky shoes and a pale pink, spaghetti strap poly nylon nightgown over that. She was carrying a noodle bowl, some soap that had glitter in it and three tubs of Valentine cookies. Girlfriend, if you are thinking of getting laid wearing that in public, you are higher than you look.

I wander over to the cheese to get some more Teleme jack because I love that shit. My friend Barky keeps yelling that it will kill me. He says it has more bacteria in it that a Jacuzzi after Fleet Week at a hooker convention. Hey, I have been eating the real non-processed Teleme cheese since I was eight and I'm still kickin'. As I'm looming over the cheese section, pawing aside lovely globes of yellow, orange and white, searching for the perfect Teleme specimen, this cute guy walks over.

Great. I hear my Mom's voice in my head, "You should never go out of the house without make-up because you never know when you might meet a nice guy." Meaning he would never look at me without makeup and nice clothes. So here I am looking like a Dinah Shore golf tour caddy. Great. Why did I even get up this morning? I get my cheese. He gets some cheese. I leave and as I head to the check out counter, guess who is in front of me? Mr. Cheese Guy. He makes a remark about my cheese. I tell him it's good and comment on his cheese. Then his boyfriend shows up with a baguette and a bottle of fabulous wine.

They pay and run off in a flurry of sunshine and rainbows and fabulous hair. I get my cheese and walk back home in a miasma of "why is it so cloudy on a sunny day" with visions of Eeyore in my head. I want to grab my ass to make sure my tail is still attached. When I get in the door I realize I forgot the meat. You remember? The flank steak was my whole reason for going in the first place. I decide just to stay put, since going out again may make my tail fall into a bush somewhere. On the up side, at least I can find the humor in the situation. Really I do.

By the way, did I tell you my cat Chauncy threw up on my shoe? He didn't mean to. He is just getting old.

EXOTIC EROTIC BALL

Hey sports fans! Well, here's the sitch. It's been nearly two years since I was laid off. I've gotten rid of my asshat boyfriend Carter, who's now so far removed from my life that he's dead to me. Honestly, dead. If he walked up to me on the street I wouldn't even see him because unlike the kid in The Sixth Sense I don't see dead people. I have been working small jobs but still haven't found anything of substance that will give me my old life back in the rollicking tech sector. I miss my old life. It was like living in the colorful Land of Oz but now I'm back in sepia toned Kansas, and I'm not happy about it. I don't look good in pigtails and gingham. No offense Kansas.

News Flash: I'm poor. Really poor. Not Oliver Twist or Tiny Tim poor but maybe that chick in An Officer and a Gentleman poor. Since I understand that one cannot exist on coffee and french fries alone, I took a job working security at the Exotic Erotic Ball and Expo at the Cow Palace. This is a seasonal event that, years ago, was called the Hookers Ball. Yes, it's all about sex, and no, I'm not wearing a g-string and pasties. I'm wearing a suit. My friend runs the security for the event and I'm thrilled to get the work. Besides I have to admit I am a bit curious. Are there really half naked men in poodle suits running about? Inquiring minds want to know.

Well this much is readily apparent, the hours are pretty brutal. Friday is a twelve-hour shift and Saturday is seventeen hours, but it's all good. This is my chance to see if the stories are true. Well after this past weekend I can tell you – those stories are pretty much all true.

If you aren't familiar with the Cow Palace in San Francisco, think of a massive grey, four-story, rectangular building shaped like a giant Bundt cake. Attached to each side, flanking it like squat wings, are two long two-story buildings. Now, take that image and age it fifty years. You see, the Cow Palace is a geriatric dinosaur that needs to be put down for its own good. It's old, musty, and falling apart in a sad, moldering way.

This "Grande Dame" of Daly City has hockey games, rodeos, dog shows and rock concerts in its glorious history. Now it plays host to a procession of near naked adults cavorting with the zeal of the Whore of Babylon on the Vegas Strip. Considering how freezing cold it gets in this building, it's a wonder so many people want to take their clothes off at all. I mean, this is San Francisco and when the wind picks up at sunset, it cuts right through you.

Friday was the Expo, and I was assigned to the vendor's gate with some fun guys. The Expo is basically a "craft fair" of sorts but with adult toys, corsets, beads, clothing - oh and Asian porn. I mean, there is white bread San Fernando Valley porn, but whenever any petite Asian gals with boobs bigger than their heads came into the vendor entrance, we would turn to each other and say "Asian Porn." Their booth was called "Asian Divas," but hell, they had monitors showing videos of Asian girls sucking dick; so what do you think they were selling?

Still, working security at the vendor's entrance was not without its perks. It was a prime area to people watch. Most attendees were perfectly normal. Housewives, plumbers, doctors, the usual but there were a few attendees who stood out big time in my mind.

The first was the "Caveman." He was a tall, skinny, white guy wearing a frizzy black stringy wig, no shirt, tennis shoes and a car shammy as a loincloth. In this getup he looked like a poor man's Howard Stern. As if it couldn't get any better than that, later in the afternoon the loincloth came off. Yup, just him and his teeny jimmy out for a stroll. He was walking around wearing that stupid wig, sunglasses and a fanny pack. A fanny pack for Chrissakes! Well, I guess he did need somewhere to keep his keys. Now, at this point, no one else is walking around naked or topless. He is the only one. It's true that during the Saturday night Ball there are body parts out on display, mostly ones you really don't want to look at, but the Expo is more reserved. Eventually we had to toss him out. What got him booted? The bondage chick complained.

It seems she was minding her own business, demonstrating a whipping post, and here comes Caveman, skulking around, leering at her. All of a sudden he grabs his microscopic jimmy and starts whacking it. This would creep out most people but Dude, when you creep out the Bondage chick, that's bad.

My personal low was the frackin' crack ho who brought four eight-year-old girls dressed as cheerleaders and expected to get them in. I have no idea if they were her children or if she picked them up from one of those glitz pageants. I told the glue sniffing hag, "Sorry, only adults 21 and over are allowed in this event." So, she left them outside, unattended, while she went in to the Expo. Are you kidding me?! What is wrong with people these days? I know this is an event that caters to a specific slice of society, but even a total moron knows you don't bring little kids to an adult event, especially one that specializes in porn.

I went into the hall to find her but found Daly City PD first. Once I explained the situation, we went went on a hunt to find her together. It would have made both of our days if we could have chucked her in jail and turned the kids over to child protective services. However, by the time we came out, she had just left with the kids. Skank.

The other jewel of the day was the Mom and Grandma wanting in with a two year old in a stroller. Ummm, 21 and OVER. Honestly, what is so hard to understand about that? Her argument was, "But he's a baby." To which I reply "Yeah and it's totally inappropriate to bring him to an adult expo that shows pornography... 21 and over. No exceptions." What is WRONG with these women?

I know, they were raised by wolverines. However, the Expo is just the warm up. The main attraction is the Ball on Saturday night, and I can assure you Cinderella never showed her face at this one. I have worked many strange events, but never before have I been asked to escort Larry Flint in his gold wheelchair, chat with Dennis Hof of the Moonlite Bunny Ranch, a legal brothel in Carson City Nevada, or park some porn magnate's new Jag. Very interesting.

I was working the VIP gate for the majority of the night, and it was cold. I'm talking well digger's ass cold. I wasn't sure if those were crystal pasties some of the ladies were wearing or if icicles had grown on their nipples. My main job was checking to make sure everyone coming in through my gate has a correct wristband and laminate card. Sounds pretty basic, right? I figured not much could beat the Caveman and the inappropriate crack ho's but as usual I failed to appreciate the capacity our society has for strange behaviour. The first was Mr. Baywatch. He was a prime example of "just because you are on a second rate television show doesn't mean you can talk your way into a VIP entrance so you can see titties for free."

So there I was, just doing my job and freezing my ass off when this guy comes up to the gate and wants to get in. I told him, "No pass, no entrance." He gets all sputtery and says, "Don't you know who I am?" I look at his non-descript ass and say, "Nope." He informs me he's on Baywatch. Really? I turn to him and say, "Well you sure as shit aren't David Hasselhoff. Honestly, who is looking at the guys on that show anyway? And you aren't Pammy Anderson or Yasmine Bleeth either, so too bad for you."

He pouts, "But I'm on Baywatch."

"Yeah... and?"

The crowd backs him up and says, "He really is on Baywatch." This is getting ridiculous. I turn back to him and tell him, "Look, you don't have a pass. If Jesus Christ himself showed up and didn't have a pass, I wouldn't let him in either, and he's my fiance. Now, here's the deal. If you were Pam Anderson I would let you in. Why? Because people in there want to see hot girls with big titties. Since you aren't a hot girl and aren't going to show off your big titties, you don't get in. Simple as that."

At that point, someone in line fishes out an extra ticket and gives it to him. He hands it to me. I hand it back to him and say, "That's great! You need to go around to the front to get into the venue with your ticket. This entrance is for VIPs with laminates only. Thank you and have a nice evening!" Score!

As the evening wore on, things became more and more strange. After midnight, various desperate people tried to scale the chain link fence and sneak in. The best was the naked guy. It seems for some strange reason, this paunchy forty-year-old man decided to take off his clothes in 45-degree temperatures and tried to squeeze in next to the chain link fence. I honestly think he was trying to "sneak up" on two gals who were standing on the other side of the fence. He probably had a mind to rub his junk on them or something. Well, things didn't go as planned. It seems he got his junk stuck in the fence. Now Mr. Frozen Naked Dude is yelling for help. The women turn, see him, point, and start laughing at him and his frozen jimmy. Daly City PD comes running up and then skids to a halt. Why? Haven't you been paying attention? Mr. Naked Guy has his junk stuck in the fence. Who wants to touch that? Not the cops I can tell you. They would need hazard pay for that job.

Technically, it was a bit of skin from his scrotum that was stuck, and since there were no volunteers to grab and release his rod and tackle, the cops were inclined to let him freeze his nuts off, literally. Well, Naked Guy is pleading and crying like a girl. One of the cops started to feel sorry for him and... kicked the fence! You heard right, he kicked the chain link fence and the jolt knocked his balls free. I think the only reason he wasn't arrested for public indecency was because no cop really wanted his bare ass in the back of his squad car. He hobbled off, gathering his shattered dignity around him, no worse for wear except for a little cut on his nut sack and a slight case of hypothermia. Hopefully this teaches him a lesson he will never forget.

We can only pray.

KILL THE IDIOTIC WORD "PLAYDATE"

I don't even remember when this phrase first came up on my radar. I don't know if it was my sister who mentioned it, or one of my many friends who have kids, or maybe I heard it from some poser soccer mom at Whole Foods. Where did they hear it? A TV show perhaps or a self-help book that is oh so popular for telling "modern" Moms how to raise their kids, which usually involves turning them into self-absorbed brats.

I have no idea when it first entered our consciousness, but let me tell you something, the word "playdate" is lame and should be banned immediately. Think about this for a moment. When we were little, and by "we" I mean anyone who is thirty or older, did we ever have "playdates?" Honestly, tell me, because I know we didn't. What did we do? We went over to a friend's house to play. Yup it went something like this, "Hey Mom, I'm going over to Nancy's after school to play!" No need to check calendars or schedules or moon phases or employ douchey pretentious terms like "playdate" that invoke pictures of a shallow woman who thinks of her kid as a pocket dog accessory and leaves the actual raising of Junior to the help while she shops at Bergdorf's and drinks herself blind.

That's what the word "playdate" means to me. It's poncey, entitled and shallow. It makes me think you really want to be those women who are bereft of conscience or humanity. Do you really want people to think you are some social climbing soulless pariah who cares more about her handbag collection than her kids? You

98

don't? Then stop using the word! It makes you sound like a douche.

Perhaps it was the hand washing monkey theory that started it! You know the theory that says if one Capuchin monkey started washing his fruit in the river soon all the monkeys would start doing it and then around the same time, other monkeys, on other islands, who had no contact with the first monkey, would start washing their fruit in the river as well?

This is what I think happens with words. It's the Capuchin monkey syndrome. Honestly, I started doing it with the word "wee." Wee means tiny, small, diminutive; just so we are all on the same page. I thought it sounded cute and well... wee, so I started using it. A lot. Guess what? People around me started using it. My theory is that one idiot social x-ray, let's call her Douche Zero, started saying "playdate" and the decline of civilization happened from there.

I would like to think we are smarter than that. I would like to think we are more enlightened. I mean, it's a new century and everything, a Brave New World but who am I kidding? We may have cool toys and Jetson's phones and Capuchin monkeys who can talk... What? You don't have a talking Capuchin monkey? Neiman's had them in their Christmas catalog! Get with the program!

Anyway, you would think we are smarter and more evolved, but we're backsliding. There actually are people out there in this day and age who think vaccinations are bad for you and cause Autism. Really? These sad souls are people who have never seen polio or smallpox up close and personal. There are people who think AIDS is a government conspiracy and wearing a tin foil hat will keep the aliens from reading your mind.

I'm just waiting for some book that tells people the sun revolves around the earth and that Goody Johnson made a cow give sour milk because she flew around with a demon in her off hours.

Honestly, do we want to go back to that?! I'm telling you, the word playdate is the first step on the slippery slope to the dark ages and I'm not going back there. Have you seen what they wore?

Enough said.

EL LOBIZON AND STRANGE MEN FROM THE MIDNIGHT MOVIES

One of the side effects to unemployment is a great deal of television watching. This invariably leads to a crash course in things hitherto unheard of in most institutes of higher learning. Today I was watching a cool show on the SciFi Channel called Destination Truth. The chiseled and handsome host, Josh Gates, travels the world investigating various oddities such as sea serpents, mermaids, chupacabras and El Lobizon.

For those of you not in the know, El Lobizon is Argentina's version of a werewolf. Only, instead of transforming during the full moon into a wolf critter, it transforms into a large dog with big ears and small kiddie arms. According to the locals, only the seventh son in a family of all boys can turn into the dreaded were-dog thingy.

The show featured this one dorkwad, I mean afflicted native, who claimed he was a Lobizon and was going to "wolf out" in front of everyone. He went through a few minutes of funny and embarrassing contortions and then pretended that he had "lost time" and didn't know about the dork dance he was doing.

This had the unfortunate effect of sending my mind reeling down the long and dusty halls of memory to a guy I once knew who was similarly afflicted. I met this guy in Los Angeles many moons ago, but that's another story. OK, twist my arm, I'll tell you now.

101

For the sake of protecting this moron's past, I'll call him El Lobo. We met at an acting job, and he seemed sane enough. Not long after we met, he divulged his deep dark secret to a few of us. He was really a werewolf. For real. He didn't look mental and this was decades before "Twilight" so having random people claiming to be lycanthropes was not an every day occurrence. He looked pretty normal, though he was really hairy. A friend of mine was dating him, and based on that intimate relationship with him, swore it was true. He really was a werewolf and he could "wolf out" at will.

Yeah, right. First I asked his girlfriend, Miss Clueless, "How do you know he is a werewolf?"
"He told me."
Wow, that's proof. Next question, "Have you ever SEEN him turn into a wolf?"
"Sort of, when we have sex he kinda wolfs out."
"What does that mean?"
"Well he gets all hairy."

Ummm, Miss Clueless, have you SEEN how hairy your current boff buddy is? He's soo hairy... (How hairy is he?) He is soo hairy that we could rub him on the shag carpet and shock half of San Francisco! Ba dum dum.

Last question, "Aren't you afraid he will infect you with his wolf cooties and turn you into a werewolf?"
"No, he's a good werewolf."

Hmmm, looking through the <u>Dungeons and Dragons Monster Manual</u> (4th edition) for Lawful Good or Chaotic Good werewolves, I find nothing. Nope, not a single good werewolf to be had. I think there is a wererabbit or something that's Chaotic Good but no werewolves. And no, we aren't counting Remus Lupin - different universe. This is real, remember?

So, my dear buddy "Van Helsing" corners El Lobo and asks him about the wolf thing. Lobo swears it's true and even offers to "wolf out" in front of Van Helsing. And here is where "reality" merged with television. Remember the Argentine guy with the contortions and stuff? Yeah, well I'm sure Van Helsing had that in mind when he replied, "No, not really because if you can do it, I'll be really freaked out, and if you can't it will just be really embarrassing, for the both of us."

He left it at that. I think if he had said, "Yes, go right ahead," he would have been treated to the dork ass wolf dance the guy did on Destination Truth.

In the interest of science, I called my brother-in-law, who is from Argentina, to get his take on this. He said the whole story is dumb, lame and no one with any brains believes it. Then again, my brother-in-law isn't the seventh son from a family of all boys. It seems the deeper I look, the murkier things get.

The moral of this story is, if someone you know tells you he is a werewolf, boot him in the junk and then run real fast in case he really does "wolf out." Oh, and tell us all about it! Next time I run into one of these losers, I want to see him "wolf out" in front of me.

I really want to film it and put it on YouTube. Ten million hits, here I come!

SELL THIS HOUSE

Things have been tight here on the ranch, so after much thought I have decided to sell the house. I mean, when I bought it I always knew I was going to sell it, especially since I have this balloon payment hanging over me. I know the economy is starting to slide, but home prices in the San Francisco Bay Area are still fairly stable compared to Squirrel Butt, AK (no offense to the amazing people of Squirrel Butt), and I should still be able to make a small profit after I pay off the bank.

I have learned you can't just throw your house on the market. It doesn't work that way. First, you need to put away all of your personal things. This means your books, pictures, dildo collection, anything that gives your house a specific personality or vibe needs to go away. You want your house to be welcoming but impersonal. Potential buyers should be able to picture themselves in your house with their own stuff and do not want to see your dildos on the mantle or the Star Wars collector plates on the wall.

The same goes for paint. I love my stylish paint colors. It is a pain in the ass, but I'm going to have to re-paint my dining room and bedroom taupe. Nice, tasteful, non-intimidating taupe. Great. I just threw up in my mouth a little, but I'll do anything to sell the house I worked so hard to buy in the first place. At this point my options are dwindling down to a few tired soldiers.

The entire process is frustrating. Sure, I heard banks sold houses to people who couldn't afford them, but I could afford the house. I had no idea that three weeks after escrow closed I would be laid

104

off. It might not have been so bad if I had a husband to share in the mortgage payment but silly me, I didn't think having a man legally attached to you was a requirement for home ownership. I feel powerless, frustrated and angry. The worst part is there is nothing I can do about it.

Thus began the Great Migration Project. Box after box of pictures, knick knacks, books, DVDs, nude images of the God Pan, and the like, are hauled down to the basement for temporary storage. I figure if I can get the house staged, on the market, sold and move within six to eight months I will be a happy camper. I know it will work. It has to. My life and sanity are really hinging on this.

I call my realtor and she puts together a whole marketing strategy: website, flyers, cards, and a prospectus, whatever that is. I have no idea, but it sounds all Wall Streety and something that Donald Trump would have. If The Donald has one, then I certainly need one as well.

We price the house at the higher end of the average price in the neighborhood. I figure this will give us negotiating room. I will accept an offer for $25,000 less, it will still be in the ball park for the average home value in my neighborhood, and I'll be able to walk away with a $20,000 profit. While that certainly is not the $275,000 profit the old lady, may she rot in Hell, made off with, $20,000 will give me a start somewhere else. I figured it was fair and reasonable.

The more I thought about it, the more I knew the best option to my money woes would be to sell the house and buy myself some breathing room. I mean, honestly, how much worse could things get? The best plan was to go into this project with hope and an air of expectation brought about by watching endless hours of reality television. If that idiot box has taught me anything, it is, "There is nothing Ty Pennington and a hoard of carpenter elves can't do with gumption, duct tape and five days."

Needless to say, things didn't go exactly according to plan. No elves showed up, Ty was MIA and this minor annoyance was the start of a full-blown nightmare.

GOLD DIGGER – LIKE A PROSTITUTE ONLY MORE ANNOYING AND NOT AS CLASSY

We have all known women like this, and frankly they just make me sad. Who am I kidding? They piss me off. Why? Because these self-centered piranhas give decent women a bad name.

Gold diggers aren't necessarily more educated than call girls, but I will say that ladies for hire are more honest. They are up front about who they are and what they do. They provide a service, a service that costs money. I can respect that.

What I don't respect are women who claim to be modern, smart, independent females and treat men like brainless penises with wallets. What makes me crazy are women, whether married or single, who make a regular habit of accepting expensive gifts from men: pricey dinners, fine wine, jewelry, clothes, shoes, cash, travel, and the like, and give them nothing in return. They figure they don't have to. I mean, after all, they just suckered some guy with a real low opinion of himself into opening up his bank account and buying them whatever they want for the pleasure of their less than stellar company. Why should they care? They think men are chumps.

At least with a high priced call girl you get a beautiful woman, her company in public and hot sex at the end of the evening. You are buying a package, and you get the whole package with no strings attached. You pay her price and she gives you the negotiated services. She doesn't ask you for an Xbox for her kid or money to send her boyfriend to France or three pairs of Jimmy Choos.

I don't like the deceit. I don't like men being taken advantage of by these poor excuses for human beings. It especially cheeses me off if they are married. I suppose if you are single, it's part of the whole "dating game," and if your mark is too dim to get that he's being played, it's just all part of love and war but a married woman? That is just wrong. Don't you care how this makes your husband feel? How disrespectful this is? You are basically telling your husband that he's a loser because he can't afford to cater to your every money-grubbing whim.

If that wasn't bad enough, what's even worse are the women who parade around, flirt with men, take all their presents and give them nothing in return. No nookie, no kiss, not even a hand job – nothing. Guys, unless you are a eunuch, that money would be better spent on a pro. You would get sex for less money, actually.

So what can we do about women like this? There are two things that work very well. The first requires men to get some balls. Listen up men out there. Knock it off! Stop giving these women gifts, cash and attention, especially the attention. Attention is like crack to these women. They will stop if there is no payday for them. They are attention whores and don't care about you at all, no matter what they say. They are lying to get their claws on your dough. Knock it off.

Second, ladies, if you know someone like this – call her on her behavior. Let's bring back the ancient art of shunning! Let them know this behavior sets women back centuries and you will not hang out with them anymore if this is how they are going to behave and then do it!

Honestly, this is the only way to stop attention whores and gold diggers in our lifetime.

MEN, TAKE NOTES, THIS IS HOW NOT TO KISS

I think the greatest tragedy known to civilized society is men who don't know how to kiss. I'm sure after the whole gold-digger rant, men worldwide are questioning their lure to the opposite sex. Here is the truth, if you are rich, you will get laid. Not only will you get laid, you can snag a "perfect ten" of a woman. There are tons of hot girls who will fall all over you, but not because they give a rat's ass about you. The fact is they want your dough. It won't matter if you can kiss or not because you are buying her stuff and she is banging the pool boy when you are at work. If you don't have a ton of dough and aren't getting dates, you need to read this.

Most men think they know how to kiss. They are as secure in their kissing prowess as they are in their ability to piss their names in the snow. However, a great many are living in a fool's paradise. To those men, guess what? You are a terrible kisser and even if your junk is huge, it doesn't matter because if you kiss like a St. Bernard, women will still dump you. Honestly. Women just don't want to hurt your feelings and tell you why to your face.

Now, they will tell your friends and their girlfriends and their gay friends and their nail gal and their hairdresser, but they won't tell you. So I'm going to help you out. Guys, put that huge ego of yours in a box and nail the lid shut. Listen to me objectively and see if you fit any of these descriptions.

Mr. Slobber - You kiss like a St. Bernard. You have a huge open mouth, lots of tongue and lots of spit all over the girls face. Does this sound sexy? It's not. If she has to wipe her face, you are doing it wrong! I'm convinced that this whole drool thing is one of the reasons that any decent hooker will let you do whatever you want for a twenty except kiss her.

Saber Tongue - A tongue isn't a weapon. Stop jabbing it in and out of my mouth like some demented whack a mole game! And get it out of my ear! That's also gross!

Brick Kisser - This guy is so afraid of intimate contact that he has his lips glued shut. It is like kissing a wall. Again not fun.

Lemon Kisser - This is the guy who has small mouth, almost like he has just eaten a lemon. He is obviously insecure and afraid to totally commit to kissing someone.

Tonsil Cleaners - Stop wiping the back of my throat with your tongue. Again - gross!

Face Eaters - Okay, stop. No really, stop! Guys that chew, lick and basically try to eat your face are weird, nasty and are in the running for "baby serial killer" of the year. This is so not sexy!

A good way to tell if a guy is a good kisser is to dance with him. If he is a shitty dancer, guess what? Nine times out of ten, he's a shitty kisser. Why? Because dancing is about emotion. Dancing is about paying attention to your partner. Dancing is about working together. Still taking notes guys? Kissing is about moving gracefully, forcefully, in rhythm, combining lips and tongues and hands in a dance. It isn't masturbation. You aren't there alone. It isn't a competitive sport. There is no single winner. If there is, then see Masturbation.

Kissing is great. Many times it can be better than sex if you do it right. How do you learn to do it right? Don't look at me, I hate teaching. I expect you to do it right the first time or there is no second time. Okay, maybe a second chance but that's it, after that you are done - game over. I'm through with continuing to date guys who are bad kissers. I hate having to avoid kissing them and missing out on one of the best parts of the relationship just because I don't want to hurt his feelings. The best thing to do (which most straight guys won't do because they will think it is "gay") is to ask a good female friend what guys you both know are great kissers and then ask them what they do.

So gentlemen, if you do any of what is on the list above, quickly hie thee to a friend for advice or a website for some pointers and change the way you kiss. Just fixing that one thing will bring you so much tail, you have no idea.

Personally, I have decided that life is too short to drink cheap wine and kiss bad kissers.

I'M LIVING IN MACY'S WINDOW

Staging your house will suck the very soul right out of your body. Sure, you think it won't be that bad. It will only be for a few months, and then you will move your things back into their rightful place. Allow me to give you a peek into my own personal Hell. Perhaps it will help you if you are ever in this situation.

I'm sure you have heard of the "Five Stages of Grief?" Well, these are my Seven Stages of Staging.

Stage One – Anger. You are resentful about having to put your things away. You are getting tired of people telling you to repaint your walls and rearrange your furniture, questioning your taste and putting a bowl of balls on your mantle. The stress of moving is bad enough without having to add to it by feeling like you are living in a furniture display in Macy's window.

Stage Two – Excitement. Now you are getting used to this a bit. While your Star Trek collector plates are in a box, the minimalist look of the house is starting to grow on you. You can deal with the chic, streamlined lack of clutter and realize there is less to clean when you have less to pull out and strew around the house like a tornado. You are realizing this will help to sell the house and then you can get your life back. You start thinking that unpacking those boxes of knick knacks in a new home will be like opening Christmas presents in July!

Stage Three – Denial. The house fails to sell in the first week but you have hope. You know it will only be a few more months and then you can move, get your life back and go on a well-deserved vacation. You can do this! You try not to look at the sliding housing market and be optimistic.

Stage Four – Anger Part Deux. The annoyance sets in. You can't find anything. You want to read that wonderful book you bought, but it's packed. You can't watch your DVDs because they're packed. You hate people calling to see the house when you are in the middle of cooking salmon and know that "food smells" are verboten. You don't want strangers touching your stuff, or looking in your closets or judging you. You just want them to go away and leave you alone.

Stage Five – Bargaining. You start stalking your real estate agent and pelting her with questions. When is the house going to sell? You can have just one more open house and someone will put in an offer. You start haunting the stacks of boxes in the basement and pull out one book or picture. You hide it between the mattresses and look at it with guilty pleasure. After two weeks, you keep it out, hidden behind a potted plant or that bowl of balls. Take THAT staging Nazi.

Stage Six – Depression. You would shoot yourself in the head if only it weren't so permanent or messy. You just can't do this anymore. You feel your sense of identity running away along with your dreams of a well-earned vacation. You feel like part of a museum display that people forgot about a long time ago. You want your things around you so bad you want to cry.

So there it is. I hope that gives you an idea of what you are in for. What happened to Stage Seven? When do you get to Acceptance? I don't know. I'll let you know when it happens. I might have to change this to the Six Steps of Staging. I don't think I will ever be accepting until it's over.

I will say, that as I sit in my staged living room, surrounded by tasteful but sterile colors and a bowl of wicker balls, it does look nice. Especially at night. The light from the wee shaded lamps on the fireplace mantel make the walls glow with a homey feeling. I tell myself, "It will only be another few months, maybe a year. I can do that!"

Yeah, just keep telling yourself that.

LET'S STICK AN ARROW UP CUPID'S ASS

Valentine's Day sucks ass. It just does, pure and simple. It's the by-product of a mafia-styled conglomerate made up of candy makers, florists and Hallmark greeting card manufacturers. It's a day filled with guilt, self-deprecation and more guilt. I can't even go out to frackin' eat on February 14th. There was this new sushi place I wanted to try, but can I go out? No. Why? Because I don't have a portable penis attached to my arm. This is a day when you can't go out by yourself under any circumstance. Couples will mock you, if they can unstick themselves long enough to notice. It's just plain stupid. It seems the main purpose of this holiday, in addition to selling chocolate, flowers, cards and wine, is to make you feel like crap. I choose not to listen to Hallmark tell me that I'm a loser if I don't have a Valentine. Shut up Hallmark! What the frack do you know?

Let's be honest. It isn't even a real holiday. I mean Valentine's Day doesn't celebrate anything historically or spiritually important. It's a capitalistic marketing scam brought to you by Hallmark cards and the florist industry. I did find this bit of info on a random website. "There are varying opinions as to the origin of Valentine's Day. Some experts state that it originated from St. Valentine, a Roman who was martyred for refusing to give up Christianity. He died on February 14, 269 A.D., the same day that had been devoted to love lotteries. Legend also says that St. Valentine left a farewell note for the jailer's daughter, who had become his friend, and signed it 'From Your Valentine.' Other aspects of the story say that St. Valentine served as a priest at the temple during the reign of Emperor Claudius. Claudius then had Valentine jailed for defying him. In 496 A.D. Pope Gelasius set aside February 14 to honor St. Valentine."

Okay, so let me get this straight. Because some religious zealot was crucified or stoned or burned or poked with sticks on a certain day, we are supposed to give cards, chocolates and pricy dinners to girls? I dismiss the "jailers daughter" scenario as apocrypha, since there is no proof this happened and most women would never admit to anything so embarrassing, and would any jailer in his right mind let his daughter consort with a religious zealot felon?

Men are on the outside of this heart shaped nightmare. For guys, the bottom line is, "It's all about sex," and there isn't anything wrong with that. Let's face it; if a sraight guy thought sex with a hot, naked woman was at the end of the Valentine's Day dinner rainbow, he would stick his head in a cow's backside.

The true center of the pain and spite for women on this day is other women. Don't let their exterior fool you. They aren't brainless fluffy bunnies wishing you good cheer and honestly inquiring after your well-being. They are velociraptors in Louboutins playing a nasty game of "mine is better than yours."

These women have a driving need to show off their trophy guy (or gal) to their friends and drink in their envy and jealousy like a fine wine. News flash girls: those of us without a partner could care less about the diamonds, the gourmet food and the La Perla teddy that was on your pillow. We aren't stupid. We know you are trying to find out one of two things: (a) how lame our partners are or (b) what it feels like to eat beans out of a can while watching re-runs of "Law & Order" on Valentine's night. Hope it gives you a good laugh, you barracuda.

I personally find Valentine's Day to be overly commercial, contrived and sexist. The woman almost never puts the same effort into her man on this day as he puts into her. I know this holiday is a huge money making scheme for companies that could care less about my love life, but I admit I'm drawn into this sick darkness anyway.

You see, the only Valentine's Day I ever spent with a man who was both available and physically present was a total disaster. It started out fine enough. I was trying so hard to be a good girlfriend. I even gave him a list of my favorite restaurants months in advance so he could make dinner reservations. I was so excited to actually be spending Valentine's with a guy. I should've gone for the can of beans and the TV.

Valentine's Day arrived and I went over to his condo to give him his card. I felt kind of dumb but it's "what you are supposed to do," so I did it. He stared at it like it was a rock from Mars. Umm, did he have a card for me? Did he write poetry that wasn't copied from Shelley or make a card with stupid lace and glitter or even just go to the mall, put out his hand and grab one? Nope. He just stared and stammered and said he didn't think he was supposed to get a card.

Dude! Did you go to public school? I mean, we had to give valentines to each and every kid in the class, or else our teacher would beat us. So, we would sit in the middle of the living room with a mimeographed list with all the kids' names, sniffing the fumes from the paper and sorting through those pre-boxed valentines. Even in third grade you knew there was a certain method to this madness. You spent a long time picking out the best, cutest card for the boy (or boys) you liked, cute cards for your girlfriends and the lamest, most unromantic cards for the dweebs you had to give cards to but didn't want to think you liked them. Remember that Simpsons episode with Lisa and Ralph Wigham and the valentine with the train that said "Choo Choo Choose Me?"

Enough said.

If you are one of those guys I may have scarred with a dorky valentine in elementary school, I'm sorry and I'm paying for it now. However, I don't think that guys really care the way girls do.

Which leads us to the second part of the Valentine's fiasco, "The Dinner." Okay, so I didn't get a card – fine. I wanted to know where we were going so I would know which cute, fun, sparkly party dress I should wear and whether I needed new shoes. Well, it seems that the list I provided was looked at as a suggestion instead of a rule. Mr. Know-it-All felt that plenty of places would have dining space the day before Valentine's Day, so he didn't bother to make an advance reservation! You can all mock me now. So there goes the great food I was imagining.

But wait, it gets better. He takes me to this hippie place that serves Pakistani food because we went there on our first date so "it would be romantic." Guess what? Not so much. Was it on the list I gave you? No. No, it wasn't. I didn't like it then, and I don't like it now. Why didn't I tell you? It's called being polite and since I wasn't asked, I couldn't give an opinion. This was the night from Hell. Guys, take a note: unless you are dating some granola eatin', hairy-legged woman who wants to eat strange tuber roots out of flat bread on Valentine's Day, understand that you will not be getting any nookie later that night.

Let's review shall we:

1) A card. Get one.
2) Reservations. Make them.
3) Dinner. It must be of more than "acceptable" quality (do not even think about fast food, weird food your date won't eat or something cheap for the sake of cheap - like the greasy spoon on the corner). Quality dinners can be cooked at home if they do not involve things you just shove into a microwave or plastic cheese. Cereal is absolutely out for a Valentine's dinner.
4) Do not get chocolates, unless the gal asks for them specifically, especially if she has been complaining about her weight lately (which is 80% of women). That's walking into the "do you think I'm fat?" trap, from which you will never free yourself. If your girlfriend looks like Kate Moss, go for it, she needs to eat the whole box in one go anyway. Just make sure she doesn't vomit afterwards.
5) Red plastic banana hammocks with hearts on them aren't sexy.
6) The same thing applies for heart shaped pubes or colored pubes. Not sexy.

7) Fun things to do (that don't cost a ton of money) are always a good idea.

I'm not even going to deal with the gay man issue. Most gay men I know eschew Valentine's Day in favor of the much more popular and practical, Beef & Blow Job Day. I think that's a more honest, practical holiday myself that more people should get behind.

I admit that I'm not very good at this Valentine's thing. I will let my first boyfriend off the hook because it was one of those young love things that burned bright and burned out just as quickly, so he never really had the opportunity to either excel or crash and burn.

Subsequent boyfriends, those that now have the nicknames of Satan, Dildo Head and Asshat, never really did anything. I'm sure you are saying, "Well if you only dated social degenerates, what did you expect? How about dating a nice guy?" Well, I actually did, and he took me to a Pakistani restaurant. I know, not all men are like that. That's very true, but in my experience all the good ones are taken or gay. I've just resigned myself to the fact that marrying Jesus is my best option.

So what does all this mean? It means I think "Beer & Blowjob Day" for men is a requirement, as long as we get our romantic dinner and La Perla teddy. I think I still have some hope left for men, but I also know I will be watching "Law & Order" tonight with the cat. I really hope all my girlfriends have wonderful evenings, just keep the details to yourselves ladies.

Maybe next year I will be one of those velociraptors in Louboutins. A gal can always dream.

WHERE THE COUGARS ROAM

Well, over a week ago, my friend Betty invited me to a country club frequented by "Men of Quality." Who might these be? You know, doctors, lawyers, judges, the usual. These titans of industry are the most regular patrons of country clubs, since they are the ones who can afford to dick around for three days trying to hit a ball around a lawn in the blazing hot sun. Betty was shilling high end golf equipment and asked me to join her.

Don't get me wrong. I like golf. It's an odd game for me to play. It doesn't have a great deal of action like roller derby or hockey. Hitting a ball around the grass seems pretty straightforward, and I was good at it in high school. I'm also good at miniature golf. While I am not great at math, I am good at figuring out which angles to use so the ball will go under the windmill and into the hole.

However, my playing style is frowned upon at a real golf course. You see, I'm a loud golfer. I dig up divots, I whack the ground with my club, and I yell choice expletives when I mess up. I'm not a good golfer in the whole sportsmanship/golf clap/drink martinis and sneer sort of way. I'm more Rodney Dangerfield from Caddyshack rather than Tiger Woods. So, I smiled, shilled clubs and did not meet any rich doctors who wanted to marry me and give me a stainless steel gourmet kitchen.

After the whole thing was over, we were hungry and decided to grab some food. We headed into Walnut Creek where I was drawn to the mystique that is Bing Crosby's. No, not the singer exactly.

This is a supper club named after the famous crooner, and it seems this establishment has a reputation as a huge cougar bar. We decide to pop in there for drinks first.

It's Thursday night, which turns out to be prime time for cougars on the prowl. Now, if you have been living under a rock and don't know the term, a "cougar" is a woman over 40, usually in her 50's, who pursues young, generally 20-something, men. Think Demi Moore and Ashton Kutcher and you know how well that turned out. So, we walked in and grabbed a seat. We order Cosmos (naturally), and I make a pass through the crowded bar, pen and paper in hand, ready to jot down any notes on cougars and their hunting habits.

Just then I see them through the tall grass of the veldt, two cougars of the tawny golden variety. At this point, my literary friends will point out that the veldt is only found in Africa and that cougars are a North American animal and to stop mixing my metaphors. Fine.

The wily cougars, seeking the higher ground of their bar stools, are peering down on their prey through the rocks swimming in their highballs. Their prey? Two unsuspecting pool boys. The cougars themselves are of the typical Walnut Creek variety. Early 50's, faces pulled back in tight lifts and the worst boob jobs I've ever seen. Is Michelangelo doing these now? Look at his female nudes - grapefruits stuck on body builder torsos. Yeah Mike, we know you liked boys but come on.

Next, two hot black guys enter the room; they start towards the plastic hags but then stop and wink at me. Well, things are looking up. I quickly and covertly check their hands for marital jewelry. No rings or ring shaped tan lines but that doesn't mean anything. Any lying dog can pocket a ring. But still, they are really cute. I stop myself and move on when I see a whiny little girl in her early 20's with a bad Prada bag knock off start to make a play for them. Yes Sweet P, we can tell the bag's fake, why even bother? Just get a regular bag. Personally, I would do many things for this cute pink Juicy Couture leather hobo bag, but sucking up to guys is not one of them.

While all of this is going on, there's a strange guy with too much hair gel, standing next to the piano player and singing "Man Eater." Damn, I can't write stuff this perfect. This guy soo reminds me of Adam Sandler in The Wedding Singer. I head back to Betty so I can take notes while I sip my drink. We have a great cocktail waitress who proceeds to fill us in on all the cougar details. She tells us she's seen it all. Some of the women are really pathetic with their tight twenty-something clothes, heavy make-up and more plastic in their bodies than Barbie. However, she says, the cougar population has declined a bit in recent months. Hmmm, I wonder if it's something in the water or perhaps the Botox?

I make a trip to the loo and find two new cougars in there, slathering on more face spackle, adjusting their too tight, two sizes too small sweaters and talking about their Botox. Ah HA! I knew that's why their faces looked so alien-like! As I exit the WC, I hear the "wedding singer" crooning "Sexual Healing." Damn, this is just too good.

Well, we decide to leave and (finally) get some food across the street, but Betty has a great idea. I should come back and really get into the scene. Get the inside scoop. Betty said she would help with my wardrobe and make-up. So coming soon - "I Was an Undercover Cougar."

I'll let you know when I work up the nerve.

MEN: THINGS YOU SHOULD AVOID IF YOU EVER WANT TO SEE A WOMAN NAKED

The stress of putting all my personal objects into boxes and hauling them down to the basement just about made me mental. Who am I kidding? It's totally made me mental, but that is considered a plus in some cultures. I know some people would look at this situation and say, "Hey, it's my stuff. These people are buying the house, not my stuff." But, it matters. In fact my mother told me she looked at a house once and never even thought of making an offer because there was a shrine to Richard Nixon in the basement. I told her, they're not leaving the Nixon shrine! She just said she couldn't live in a house like that because she would be seeing the Nixon shrine in her head every time she went downstairs. Point taken.

So I boxed up my personal pictures, put away my Bill Clinton biography, and wrapped the fine art piece my cool lesbian friend made that looks like a ... flower. Yeah, that's it. It's a flower, but it's going in the box anyway.

As I packed, my mind wandered off to strange places full of cobwebs and impressionist paintings and rabid Cujo dogs. I thought about the sterilization of my house, the removal of any small memento that defines me as a person and the collapse of my whole life in general. So many people define themselves by their job, and I've come to the conclusion that this is fucked up. Honestly, it's totally unhealthy; especially when it stops you from growing in a new direction. I mean, what if I wasn't meant to work in the tech industry? Maybe I was meant for other things? Bigger things. Better things! I attacked a box of pictures with a new vigor. I was going to have a new purpose in life. I was going to sell the house, make a little money, take a trip to England, meet Alan Rickman and then my life would be perfect.

That's when I started finding "the pictures." You know the ones. The snap shots of failed relationships you just shove in a box, forgotten about until they bite you like a snake when you flip over a rock. At the time, I thought some of these relationships might have worked out. Unfortunately, none of these guys ever took basic How To Deal With Women 101.

With this thought in mind, I feel that hapless men need to be given a clue, since they are obviously too bereft of cash and good sense to buy one.

So here, I'll even share a few of them with you. Guys, write these down and tape them over the toilet so you will see them often.

1) Don't be a gross slob. Learn how to eat with a knife and fork. Believe me, there is a right way and a wrong way. Learn what they are, practice and choose the right way. Here is a hint; the correct way does not involve grabbing your fork in your fist. Do not eat with your mouth full. Belching the alphabet at the table (or anywhere) will not get you laid. It will get you shown the door or the couch. Likewise, farting with pride and remarking on it. Ladies understand everyone has bodily functions. We just don't want to be subjected to a constant barrage of them. We would personally die of horror if you ever for a minute thought that we fart.

2) Get some better lines that do not include anything vulgar, infantile or misogynistic. Phrases used on a lady should never include, "Cram Your Deal," "Butter Your Biscuit" or "Pimp Your Ride." Let me say, in a state of extreme humiliation for having to admit this, I've heard all of these. Let me also state that none of these has ever worked and in fact had the opposite reaction. Say this to a lady and she will put you in the "I would not go near you if you were the last man on Earth, the world was covered in piss

and you lived in a tree" category. Guys, you are not being funny, you are being offensive.

3) Don't be cheap. We hate cheap. This doesn't mean you should pony up the steak and lobster for a chick who will eat your food, drink your wine and give you the boot since she's having hot monkey sex with another guy later that night. It happens. Really. What I am saying is don't give me a laundry list of why you need to pinch every penny until it screams and why you think that eating at Red Lobster is a rockin' special occasion. I can be frugal. I know what it's like to go through rough patches, but there is a difference between frugal and cheap.

4) Don't talk 24/7 about your old girlfriends. We don't care. Honestly, we don't, and the more you keep talking about them the more we are thinking, "Then why don't you just go back to Binky/Twinkie/whatever the bimbo's name is and leave me alone with my Xbox which is infinitely more exciting than you."

5) Don't promise what you can't deliver. If you say you are going to call, call. If you say you are going to bring me a pressie to make up for doing something stupid, then you better make with the gifty. If you tell me you are going to become Mayor of Stockton and marry me, then follow up. By the way, if Chris York from 3rd grade at Colonial Heights is out there, I want to know if you are Mayor yet and is our engagement still on? If not, I have other guys in the wings. I mean, you did push me in the boy's bathroom and offer to take me to Dairy Queen on the back of your bike as a date. I slapped you across the face for being fresh and trying to kiss me. That is when you proposed. Hmm, maybe I am going about this all wrong as an adult.

6) Really - don't say "Cram Your Deal." It's just gross.

7) Shower. Smelling like a man is fine. Smelling like a hoard of monkeys stuck on a marine base on a tropical island with a bar and shore leave is NOT okay. Personal hygiene is important.

8) Smoking is nasty. Unless it's an occasional good cigar and I get one too.

9) If you have killer foot odor (and you know if you do) do not under any circumstances take off your shoes. I have a cousin who can clear a room. His foot odor is a weapon of mass destruction and if we could export that, we would have been done with this stupid war in Iraq twenty four hours after it started.

10) Re-read and commit to memory all of the above. Really guys, I'm just trying to help you out.

That concludes my Public Service Announcement for the day. I really hope this has helped a few of you guys out there.

THE FOOLPROOF FLAMING BOWL DRINKS PLAN

I never cease to be amazed by the weirdness my life attracts. So, you will recall that the last time I had a night of trying to keep up with the boys in the drinking arena, I woke up trashed and smelling like ass. I promised myself I would never do that again. At least until I had a better plan. Well I found one and while it was strange, it was mighty. A mighty strange plan.

My friend Dave was back in town. He works in the technology sector and has been traveling to Silicon Valley quite frequently on business. When he's in town, I try to get together with him and Jason because two guys are better than one. Honestly, I like to think that I'm the civilizing influence that keeps them from spitting on the sidewalk, jumping up to smack awnings or pissing their names in the snow. Not like we have snow, but they could piss their names on the sidewalk, which would be even worse. I'm also handy as a mascot, and I can find their keys when they have forgotten where they left them.

As most women have realized by now, our vaginas also function as a tracking device enabling us to find lost keys or spare change just by moving it in a slow arc and waiting for the pinging noise. No really! Ladies, haven't you tried this at home? Unfortunately it doesn't work on my keys, just other people's keys. I think it's biological.

So, this time I had a foolproof plan to keep things civilized and stop me from singing bad versions of Kevin Barry. First, Dave picked me up and we drove to one of Jason's favorite eateries, The Townhouse, in Emeryville. Not only do they have great food but they also have some of the best mojitos around. I love the fact that they muddle the mojitos from scratch.

Dave and I got there right after Jason and joined him at the prohibition-styled copper topped bar. We got our mojitos, then ordered garlic fries and a few sliders. You see, the foundation of the plan was getting food early. I figured a good meal of fat and animal protein would act as a buffer between the booze and our livers. The mental picture of booze bubbles bouncing off a protective layer of french fry grease made me happy and gave me a false sense of security. The fact that our last night out also started with garlic fries was not a big enough sign for me. This time it would be different. This time I had a foolproof plan. Foolproof I tell you!

We ate our food, drank our drinks, debated getting another round but thought better of it. The night was still young and we had a great deal of perfect fun planned. No sense running too fast for the finish line. That's what amateurs and college students do. We're adults, we've learned to pace ourselves. We decide to head over to Jason's condo a few blocks away, stumbling distance really. He had something to show us, and our stomachs were already buffered by a layer of cow and fat.

Jason's place is like most single man caves. There's stuff everywhere, though Jason does have a preponderance of books, book shelves and weaponry, namely swords. He also has a grand piano, so I guess that makes him a classy boy bear with furniture. Dave doesn't have this problem. Dave has a wife. She makes sure the house is not a man cave, except for the specifically designated area with pool table and big screen television.

So, we started out at Jason's place with everyone's favorite, whiskey. 21-year-old scotch whiskey in a fancy enameled bottle to be exact. I have no idea who made it, but the bottle was pretty and it was yummy so what more do you need? We grabbed a handful of crackers or mints or whatever it is that we found in the couch to snack on. At least I know it wasn't spray cheese since I can attest to the fact that Jason doesn't use spray cheese. Other weird things like spray pancake batter, yeah, but not spray cheese.

By the time we finished our shots of whiskey, it was early enough to go have cocktails at my favorite place, the Forbidden Isle. What is the Forbidden Isle? It's just about the best Tiki bar on the planet! It's over in Alameda, and I've been telling Dave about it for years. Now I get the opportunity to show him why these are the best flaming bowl drinks and frosty cups of love on the planet.

You see? This was my foolproof plan! We get greasy food, eat appetizers we find in Jason's couch and then have flaming bowl drinks in my favorite bar. There are no karaoke losers in this bar. There is a bathroom so I don't have to wander the cold streets with an exploding bladder, and there are no Irish Car Bombs. Well, technically I guess they could make some, but when you are surrounded by frosty tropical goodness, why bother ordering anything else? People who come to the Tiki bar and just order a beer piss me off. It's like flying to Paris and going to McDonald's. Why don't you live a little outside your comfort zone?

We took two cars so Dave could get back to his hotel afterwards. Jason knew where he was going, so I went with Dave to navigate and make fun of his talking GPS unit. It has a computerized female voice that reminds me of a spa attendant in a galaxy far, far away. "Turn. Left. In. Thirty. Feet." She speaks in that mechanical way that makes every word its own sentence. I suppose since she's a machine she can be forgiven for sounding like one. That doesn't mean I can't make myself look ludicrous by making snarky comments to the GPS.

The Forbidden Isle isn't large. In fact, it's fairly cozy as far as bars go. There are about a dozen stools at the bar, four booths that seat four in comfort or six if you're skinny or really friendly. It also has a seating area with some couches, Don Ho chairs and low coffee tables. Once we arrive at the bar, we snag a fishing net swagged booth and order frosty adult beverages. I have to start with my favorite, the Chamborlada. It's a pina colada with a float of Chambord and an orchid. Yes, a fresh orchid. It's pretty and girly and I can put it in my hair. I have no idea what frosty beverage the men ordered. I was too focused on sucking mine through a straw like my life depended on it.

We decide to order some deep fried munchies because another layer of grease will definitely keep me from jumping on the table later, singing the tune to the original Hawaii 5-0 and pretending to surf. So, everything was going according to plan until the plan all of a sudden hit a rock and jumped the tracks. It seems the Tiki bar now has a new way to make you their slave. Rum flights. The last time I was here with my friend Captain Black, we discovered these rum flights, their large selection of premium rums and the card they keep on file. If you drink one of each of the rums listed, you get a plaque with your name on it or a parade or wee Hula girls with flaming batons dancing around you. Well, the boys discovered the rum and I had to keep up. Can you see the holes in this foolproof plan?

Our server retrieved my rum flight card and got new cards for the guys. We started with a trip of the Caribbean islands. Each flight contained four shots of rum. By the way, I should also say that the frozen drinks are yummy and deadly. When combined with rum, I was feeling no pain. I started looking for my surfboard. The boys loved the rum flights, they thought they were great. They scarfed down sweet potato fries, crab cakes and rum with no effect. I started eyeing the fishing net and wondering if I could actually surf on the bar. Fortunately my better nature kicked in, or... that might have been Jason kicking me under the table.

At least I knew that singing Kevin Barry would not be appropriate for the venue. I decided to make a sedate retreat to the ladies room where I could sing "Yellow Polka Dot Bikini" to the various smiling hula girls adorning the wall of the john. When I returned from the ladies room, AKA my private recording studio, I saw the guys had ordered crab Rangoon and a flaming bowl drink. I mean, how can you turn down a bowl of flaming juice and booze with foot long straws in it? You can't.

I have no idea how long we were there. Time ceases to have any meaning when you are breathing through a straw. I know it was past the late night news but before closing time. Dave drove me home and waited until I got inside. I suppose in case aliens decided to abduct me or maybe he was curious if I was going to bazooka barf off the balcony.

Sorry to disappoint you, but there was no barfing to be had. I got inside, fell into bed and slept the sleep of the drunk and the righteous. When I woke up, I was a little slow moving but other than that, I wasn't too bad off. It bummed me out having Chauncy here to judge me. There are a few things cats are very good at and recrimination is one of them. While I was still somewhat alert, I saw the fatal flaw in my foolproof plan.

I'm going to have to re-think the plan before I do this again.

FAKE NIPPLES

Yes, you heard me correctly, fake nipples. I first saw these tantalizing tidbits on a <u>Sex and the City</u> episode. Samantha (of course) was enraptured by them, while I thought this was the strangest idea ever. Silicon nipples you stick over your own nipples so you can walk into a room and have high beams. I guess this is supposed to be a better magnet for picking up men than smelling like bacon.

If you think I am making this up, I'm not - <u>www.bodyperks.com</u>. Their website proclaims that they are the original nipple chicks and are all about nipple enhancement. The site also says, "The possibilities for fun are endless! Whether you're out on the town or playing volleyball, bodyperks comfortably stay in place and give you the added attraction of playful, fun breasts."

Let me get this straight. My breasts now need to be playful? Since when? The nipple slingin' site also boasts comments from typical "Girls Gone Wild" wanna-bes of how these made all the difference in their quest to make out with every guy in the bar. Frankly, I have zero desire to make such a spectacle of myself. I'm far too picky for that. You go, Skankarella! You might even hook up with an "aspiring hip hop star" still living in his parent's basement!

Perhaps I am wrong, but I thought we all started wearing bras so we didn't show high beams and poke people's eyes out at the office or the subway or in the grocery store line. I thought pointy nipples in public made us look cheap or slutty or like freaky hippies. When did this change? Do we want to see huge, pointy nipples in a PTA meeting, at the office, in line at the post office? Are they that distracting?

I am truly perplexed. You see, for me personally, I've never had flat nipples. Let me check again just to be sure. Nope, they look like the silicon ones they are selling for $20. Do some women have flat, non three dimensional nipples? I don't know. Honestly. It's just me here. Well, me and my Xbox 360. There's not even a new Welsh Corgi puppy (HINT HINT) to keep me company. I'm not counting the old cat who's looking at me as if I've lost my monkey mind.

Do women really want these and, most importantly, what do you do with them? Let's say you get lucky. You have infatuated some guy with your prominent nipples and you are going to get naked. How do you keep him from seeing two circles of silicon stuck to your breasts? Ladies, you know we plan all kinds of "trips to the ladies room" to disguise a myriad of sins we don't want guys to ever find out about. Now, on <u>Sex and the City,</u> Samantha deftly swiped them off with a pass through the dress and tossed them over her shoulder before the "great reveal." It was a slight of hand worthy of Houdini or Criss Angel.

However, that's TV. You know what would happen in real life? The nipples would stick. They are designed to stick. You couldn't gracefully swipe them off. The guy would think you were nuts and wonder what the hell you were doing? It would be too humiliating to fess up to the fact that you reeled him in with silicon falsie nubs.

What if there are trace amounts of spirit gum remaining? How do you explain that? How about if you do have flat nipples and you manage to get rid of the "man lures" and the guy finds out the real ones do not resemble the lures he was drawn in by? Now what do you do? It's the female equivalent of the cucumber down the pants. Not like we ever fell for that but...

Another problem, what if the sticky stuff used to attach the nipples fails? What if you are at a party and one nipple is perky and in place, being playful and playing croquet while the other one is heading East with a bit of a Southern Slide. Yeah, that's real attractive! I guess I will never know for sure unless someone ponies up the $20. We can pass them around and decide for ourselves. Maybe we can make a demo and put it up on YouTube.

Or not.

FRUGAL IS THE NEW CHIC

Yes, it seems that poor is in. Now that the Depression has arrived, thanks to idiots who are still living in their mansions, summering in the Hamptons, and spending hundreds of thousands on their "girls gone wild" daughters' weddings, complete with lobster dinners and gold plates, we are discovering the joys of government cheese.

I just read an article that proudly touted how the rich were cutting back on their excursions to Rodeo Drive. Cutting back how, you may ask? Well, their idea of cutting back is buying only one Chanel sweater instead of eight and asking for plain non-logoed bags to carry their purchases in. Evidently the Hollyweird elite are just now coming to the conclusion that sporting their myriad of label bags when people are standing on line for a free Grand Slam at Denny's, may be rubbing it in just a tad. Don't worry. The majority of them are still shallow, talentless, morally bankrupt shells that honestly just don't care.

It's just that frugal is chic now. It's the new black. These barracudas are just waiting with baited breath for the upswing when they can haul out their $20,000 diamond collar for their shivering pocket dog instead of having to go with the Italian leather one from Prada. Very understated you know.

If that wasn't enough, I was reading an article in the financial section of the San Jose Mercury News, a major paper in my neck of the woods. This article made me want to grab the reporter and smack her. Just one good smack to wake her up. This article did not belong in a major publication, especially in the financial section. A supermarket rag? Yeah, definitely. The Pennysaver? Why not? But not the financial section.

Anyway, I thought this article was going to be about unemployment numbers, how to make yourself more marketable, or where the best government cheese is to be found, but no. It was about how sad it is that this reporter's friend, who is divorced with one kid, has been collecting $20,000 a month in vaginamony, for the past three years, and how little it is!

It seems, according to the article, this woman has played at running a dress business for the past four years that has never turned a profit. Now she might have to get a real job because the ex has been laid off and is looking to turn off the gravy train. Oh, how horrible! What is she going to do if she loses her paltry 20k a month? How is she going to pay the $12,000 mortgage on her McMansion and have enough for her kids' private school tuition and her pilates classes?

Umm, WTF? Okay, what could everyone out there do with $20k a month? Jesus, that's looking close to what I'm making in a year now. Let's do the math – that's $240,000 a year without working! I know some of you might consider just being in her marriage as working for the annuity she is now receiving but, I don't buy it. I mean, if her husband was the Creature from the Black Lagoon, maybe, but somehow I sincerely doubt that's the case.

So what should poor Miss "I have no money" do? Here is my cunning plan:
1) Sell your house. I'm willing to bet it's worth at least 4.5 mil. Take $2 mil and call it a day.
2) Put your kids in public school.
3) Sell the business, because obviously you are not good at it.
4) GET A JOB.

I know, I know. I can hear the excuses now. The housing market sucks, public school sucks, I'm not trained to do anything except suck off of rich men and take yoga class. Guess what? LEARN. I am so tired of the entitled whiners. I think it would be character building to live a little like the rest of the unwashed masses.

After all, poverty is the new black! Haven't you heard?

HELP! I'VE STUMBLED INTO A CULT INSURANCE INTERVIEW AND CAN'T GET OUT!

I'm still looking for a job, still sending resumes into the black hole of doom, still trying to get a face-to-face interview and it's frustrating. Well, yesterday I glimpsed some light at the end of the tunnel. Unfortunately, it turned out to be a train. Why? I'll tell you. I got a call for an interview. It was only my second interview in six months. The lady on the phone led me to believe that the position was for an Executive Assistant job in Concord. This could be the lead I've been waiting for, so I get there at 10:10 in the AM, walk into the lobby and find ten people sitting around, all filling out applications. I think, "Well, maybe they need an admin in addition to whatever mass cattle call thing is going on."

I'm not a snob but omygod, some of these people hurt my eyes. One gal had this frizzy Jersey hair perm, a white polyester top and skirt (with a large stain on the back), strappy sandals with a heart charm and a gold glitter hooker bag.

Me? Black Ann Taylor suit, white shirt, cute black Biviel shoes, nice conservative bag (Nine West, not the stuffed animal bag that my friend Pasha hates so much). I get called in to talk to some young guy in an ill-fitting suit. He takes me to his office, tells me there are three interviews for this position. He then asks me five softball questions, tells me I've passed the first interview and will go directly to the second.

I'm not taken to some higher up's office but to a big room with other people - including Jersey Hair. There are dry erase boards all over the place with info and slogans like:

Success Formula
32-36 appointments
24-28 presentations
4 full days in the field
door knocks - referrals - work smart
Failure Formula = (20-15) (17-14) (3)

Is this some abstract Moonie math? We have to fill out a six-page feel good survey with questions like, "Would you ask directions if you were lost?" There is new age jazz playing and they have water, coffee and donuts (which I can't eat). This is not looking like an Executive Assistant interview. How do I get out of here? Are they going to kidnap us? Even if I can get out of here, after whatever time share horror we are going to have to sit through, it's still going to be hours of my life I will never get back. Hours I could have spent applying to Pixar.

None of the women in the room could work for any C-level executive the way they are dressed. I was told to dress business corporate. They are dressed Dairy Queen counter. The only thing keeping me sane is making notes in my moleskine so I can write about this later, or as evidence at trial if we are all found murdered.

I got here at 10:10 AM, and now an hour later this guy starts talking. It seems this job is to sell insurance to various union members. This company is the one labor unions use, and we are to call members who have policies, get paperwork signed and see if we can add on extras to their policy, such as funeral expenses. There are tons of people there to give testimonials on how they have worked anywhere from a year to five years with the company and are making 70k - 200k without yearly bonuses. The President guy, who is now a consultant, retired at forty-five and is now forty-eight. He claims he used to be a rock band manager and sound engineer for Led Zeppelin and Steppenwolf, among other bands.

God, do I really want to sell insurance? Can I do that? Could it give me my life (and finances) back? I don't know. This is so screwed up. I am so confused. I don't know anything anymore. After the nearly two hour talk, I am sent back to manager #1's office. He asks me what I thought. I told him it was interesting, but I thought I was there to interview as an Executive Assistant. I told him the gal on the phone didn't explain what this position was exactly for. Sure, I assumed that was the position since my resume I posted on-line was my admin one. He told me they would be calling people back this afternoon for the last interview. I shook his hand and drove home.

It's now 4:04pm and the phone hasn't rung once. Big surprise. I could have said, "Wow! Fantastic! Sign me up!" and got the third call for sure, but I knew this wasn't for me. The whole vibe was a little Scientologist freaky. The question now is, am I letting a six figure salary slip away? I don't know. I had to be honest with myself and this just sounded too good to be true. We all know what happens when things sound too good to be true. They usually are.

I'm bemoaning the fact that I wasted a huge chunk of my day, and all I really want is a non-judgmental donut with sprinkles or coconut. Maybe tomorrow I will go into the City and get shoes or some more clothes. My pants are an inch looser in the waist. It sucks that the only job hit I've gotten in four months was this freaky cult insurance thing. So far this month I've sent out fifty two resumes.

Sigh Does anyone work at Pixar or Google, and are they hiring?

DON'T STAND NEXT TO YOUR NAKED NEIGHBOR

I suppose a little back-story is in order here. My house sits above my garage so the living area is 1 1/2 stories above ground level. My house also has windows, tons of windows. The living room has seven windows, the dining room has three, the kitchen has one, the bathroom has one, the sunroom has three and the bedroom has two. I've don't have any curtains in the dining room, kitchen or sunroom.

Why does this matter, aside from my neighbor, the Unhappy Cow, who lives in the flat on the west side of the house and gives me grief for having my dining room lights on? Because on the East side, Splash Poo Mansion is also 1 1/2 stories high, so we face directly into each other's rooms. The cow gets the light from my dining room, Splash Poo Mansion gets to see into my bedroom, and I get to see into the majority of both their houses. At least I'm seeing the common areas and not their bedrooms.

To be honest, I tend to walk around naked quite a bit. Hey, it's a free country and I'm lazy. However, having my neighbors get a peek for free is not something I want to encourage so I put curtains up in the bedroom. Believe me, they are getting the better end of the naked deal. Sure, I'm not twenty anymore, but have you seen my neighbors? I thought not.

The other day, as I was pulling my bedroom curtains, I happened to look across the way into Splash Poo Mansion's dining room/living room. Sure, in the past I saw cats, cats, more cats, crap

141

(literally), junk, shit, stacks and stacks and piles of books and boxes and paper and other things too strange to identify. Then, into this chaos strides Mr. Mansion in the full-on glory of nature, swinging his nether wallop and workin' what God gave him.

In the Biblical tradition, I was struck blind.

Flash forward one week. I am walking home from my soul draining temp job. It takes me about twenty minutes from desk to door to get home. I'm crossing the street over by Whole Foods when I see someone coming up the street towards me holding a PC monitor and panting (so would I, if I were lugging a monitor for a mile). I see it's Mr. Mansion.

Great. What do you say to a neighbor who has probably glimpsed you naked (or near so) and you have (recently) seen him naked in all his scary glory? Do you even acknowledge his existence? I'll answer that question. No, definitely not! You just pretend not to see him, keep your designer glasses on and carry on a pretend conversation on your cell phone. I let him huff ahead of me with the monitor, wait for him to go into the house, then call Ruthie, and in hushed tones explain what just happened and how I was traumatized all over again. Ruthie wants to know why I'm whispering, since I'm inside the house, then proceeds to talk me down out of the tree like she normally does.

I wonder if this is one of the signs of the coming of the Anti-Christ. I should look that up. I am near convinced that it is.

THE GREAT CRASH OR HOW WE WERE ALL SCREWED OVER WITHOUT A KISS

This day has been coming for quite some time, but we all tried to ignore it. We thought if we didn't slow down long enough to look at the train wreck, it would go away. We hoped people's better natures would prevail. We prayed that the out of control greed, on a scale not seen since the railroad robber barons of old, was a thing of the past.

We were wrong.

I realized the housing market was in a slump, but how was I to know that a bunch of criminal buttmunches would rape the middle class and fly off to the Hamptons? I can just see them on their private planes, laughing and burning hundred dollar bills as jet fuel, while we slide into poverty, bad reality television and government cheese.

I would personally like to thank Angelo Mozilo, co-founder of Countrywide (my mortgage lender), Phil Gramm, Chairman of the Senate Banking Committee (thanks for deregulating laws that have been in place since the Depression to keep this shit from happening again), Bernie Madoff for his $50 billion Ponzi scheme, Dick Fuld of Lehman Brothers who proved you can make $500 million selling nuclear waste disguised as investment bonds, and of course Hank Paulson for selling us the big bailout mess. If I could, I would take away every toy they own, pelt them with rotten eggs and make them stand on a street corner in the Financial District with a sign that says, "You are fucked because of me. Have a nice day."

Don't think I've forgotten the biggest piece of this pie, the largest contributor to our problems, the American Consumer. Yes, all of us have to take a big bite out of this shit sandwich. Admit it, you thought puppies were raining from the sky. The streets were paved with gold and it didn't matter if you couldn't afford that 90" plasma TV. You could just pull out your piece of plastic and take it home. Why buy a reasonable, modest house when you could have an eight bedroom McMansion with all the add-ons? You too can have a Great Room, cathedral ceilings, crown molding and a media room - especially since you bought that gigantic television. You can watch the play-offs from outer space now!

Some of us spent like the world was ending tomorrow, and some of us bought within our means but had our jobs disappear before our eyes. Either way, we're all in the same boat. It's just that a few of us get to have that look of self-satisfied poverty on our faces. I know, I see that look in the mirror. It's the look that says, "We all may be eating at the dollar store but at least I didn't buy all that worthless crap." That's usually the cue for one of the over spenders to offer to screen a DVD on their huge high-def television before the bank repos it. How do you say no to that?

I try not to judge. It's hard, but I try. I may not have bought the plasma screen but I do have something that's made me the envy of many men. It's the thing college boys have in dorm rooms, what single men would want behind closed doors and what divorced men do trying to re-claim their lost youth and sense of self. It's not a thing a married man has because usually his wife won't let him. It's... a fridge in the living room stocked with beer.

Yes, in my effort to distract myself from the fall of the Roman Empire, and the fact that I've still to find a permanent job, I've decided to replace an end table with a small dorm fridge and stock it with gay beer, cider and gin. I can reach it from the sofa when I am watching TV. I can also reach it when I set up a chair in front of a monitor for my PS2. Gaming is thirsty work especially when playing Rock Band or Final Fantasy. I've found it's always a good idea to have cold gin for Batcave martinis on hand. So why did I do it? Why not? Right now I am in the middle of end of year cleaning and have decided to scrub each room in turn. This has resulted in the living room becoming a staging area for the regurgitation that is my life. I deserve a beer damnit!

There are a few females of my acquaintance who disapprove of the "man fridge." They don't find it lady-like and think it will drive men away in droves. Really? I would think, next to rubbing my body with bacon, this is the biggest man magnet there is. I asked my fiancé, the Big JC, about the fridge and he was okay with it. He figured if God didn't want you to have refrigeration on demand, we would all be living in Sweden, the Land of Ice and Porn, not that there's anything wrong with that. God likes Sweden, especially the ice bars and curling competitions. Curling is forty-two flavors of awesome.

The only downside I can see is having all your beer on display in the event that hordes of riff-raff storm your house uninvited. You can always hide booze in out of the way corners, but a fridge in your living room is akin to pouring blood in the water off the Australian coast. Jaws always shows up. The parasites swarm in, drink your booze, eat your food, piss on your rug, impregnate your dog and leave.

Wow, that just sounded like the banking reprobates who are responsible for my life situation in the first place.

Now I'm really feeling the train wreck of our country's pain.

WHY MY FIANCE THINKS THIS SUCKS

For those of you who haven't been paying attention or are still traumatized by the thought of Mr. Splash Poo Mansion's member, allow me to introduce you to my fiancé, Jesus, also known as Savior, Lord and my personal favorite – the Big JC. You have no idea...

Well, we were chatting the other day, after Mary Magdalene went out for a hookah break, and the subject of houses of worship came up. You see, Oakland has a new church; The Church of Christ the Light. Actually it's a cathedral. You would never know it by looking at it though. To me, a cathedral is an inspiring architectural masterpiece of wood and stone and stained glass and flying buttresses, (whatever they are – I've heard Notre Dame has many) but this looks like a World War II bunker. It's all concrete and grey and boxy and ... well... bunker like. The actual "church" part is a huge thingy. Really, a thingy. Not a spire or a dome or any easily identifiable shape.

Wait, my fiancé is reminding me that it resembles one of the parts he made out of Adam's rib. It's a yoni! Yup, a glorious glass va-J-J. Now, first, you may ask, what is the The Church of Christ the Light and how did it raise the tens of millions of dollars necessary to build a Stalinist bunker of a church topped by a glass peesch? I looked it up on the Internet, because it's not just for porn anymore, and found ...the Catholics. Yup, it's a Catholic church. Figures. The Church is retooling itself, and this is their modern answer. A "cathedral" that enfolds many small neighborhood churches in its Mothership embrace. It's a little like the Borg in that way. You will be assimilated. It has underground parking, offices, a mausoleum (no lie), a learning annex and (this is the best part) a memory garden designed by and for people molested by priests.

You know something, (and the Big JC is agreeing with me on this one) I think a memory garden is a piss poor answer to the huge molestation issue that has been perpetrated by a minority of priests. I'm thinking if I had been molested, a garden in a bunker is small recompense for my wrecked life and stolen childhood. I think prison is the first thing the Church should think about. Yup, turn all of those deviant monsters over to the DA for a trial then offer to give their victims fifteen minutes alone with them in a room with a dull butter knife.

But I am diverting myself from the main issue here and what my fiancé thinks really bites – the money. Do you really need to spend tens of millions of dollars on an ugly building to worship God? God doesn't need your money, and whether your God is male, female, both, neither, a cat or a head of cabbage named Ralph, she/he certainly does not need you to spend all that money and on what?

How about meeting in small communities like you used to and raising money to feed the poor? Why don't you clothe the naked (especially some of those people in Berkeley or my neighbor) and ease the suffering? You know, all that stuff the Big JC was preaching oh those many years ago in a dusty desert that's now overrun in blood and not so much by "love thy neighbor?"

Don't you think that money could have been put to better use, especially in these tough economic times? Do you really think God cares about your cement temple to your own vanity? Honestly, think about that, because as I said before God doesn't need it. She told me.

Well then, JC got all pissed, pontificated for an hour on the vanity and greed that is man, threatened to start over with cockroaches, then made himself some wine and chilled out. I believe it was a nice Pinot Grigio.

So there it is. I walk by it every day on my way to my temp job and I just keep thinking, "Do you really think this brings you closer to The Divine?"

THE SQUIRREL STOLE MY THONG

The fact that this actually happened to me proves that both squirrels and thongs are evil. What am I talking about? Have I lost my mind? Did my government cheese go bad?

I've been looking for work, really, I have, but the process is a lot different now in the digital age and a lot more frustrating. You don't get to talk to people or follow up with phone calls. You send resumes into the electronic black hole of doom and hope for the best. I once had a temp job in the HR department of a white-collar firm. They were actively seeking someone to fill the position. They told me to put the resumes I received in a folder so they could look at them later. The resumes kept coming in, and I would put them in the folder. The folder kept getting larger and larger. Finally, I asked when they wanted to look through this veritable tidal wave of office experience. They told me the resumes were probably too old, to throw them all out and start over. So now I know what is happening to those black hole resumes. If a company gets too many responses, they just chuck the lot in the trash and start over. Great.

As fate would have it, I was so caught up in sending out resumes and, let's face it, playing video games, that I ran out of clean underwear. I don't have a working washer/dryer since the cranky old woman who sold me the house, may she rot in Hell, foisted that broken piece of shit on me. Do you want to know how long it takes for a full tub of water to evaporate from a washing machine? Three years! How do I know this? I know this because it turned into an unintentional science experiment in my basement.

149

You see, I was so excited when I heard that a washer/dryer came with the house. After a dozen years of using the laundromat, this was a huge deal. As soon as I signed the papers and got the keys, I brought all of my laundry over. That's right, before the furniture was even moved I wanted to wash clothes in my own washing machine. Everything started out fine. It started to wash the clothes, but I soon found out the water wouldn't drain. So there were my clothes, marinating in a soup of soapy, dirty water.

I fished everything out, wrung out my clothes in the sink and put the clothes into the dryer. Guess what? You got it. The dryer didn't work at all. My only option was to take my wet clothes and hang them around the backyard on various branches to dry. In the meantime, there the water stayed, turning stagnant, in the drum of the washing machine. It was too gross to bail out, so I just waited for it to go away, and that's how I know it takes three years for a full load of water to evaporate.

What does this have to do with not having clean underwear? Well, now I've got to take my clothes to the laundromat, and if you don't show up first thing in the morning on a weekend, you have to deal with all the mothers and their dozen screaming kids. They take up all the machines and their kids get the chairs all sticky.

Since I missed my window of opportunity, my last resort was washing batches of undies in the sink and hanging them out on the back porch rail to dry, white trash style. Sue me. So my underwear is now steaming on the railing of my deck. Yup, steam is coming off them because I washed them in hot water and its cold outside. Hell, it's early morning, it's supposed to be cold. I thought underwear washing would be a simple chore but I'm wrong, as usual. I start to go back inside when I see something move out of the corner of my eye. A flash of brown, fluffy tail. What now?

I turn around and freeze. There, on the rail of my deck, is the Evil One. Yup, the hefty lemon lobbing rodent is back, and this time that squirrel, that rat with superior fashion sense, has my lavender silk La Perla thong in his rabid little mouth. I know I said thongs are evil, but at one time I thought if it was expensive enough, maybe it would be comfortable. This one is not my most comfortable thong, but it is the most expensive. It cost an entire day's pay, and now it's being carried away by that little disease ridden beast! I turn quickly to grab the nearest weapon to hand, pull a muscle in my skull and yell out in pain. You know the pain I'm talking about? There is some strange muscle or nerve that runs from the top of your head, across your skull and down your neck. When you turn your neck too fast, it shoots red-hot daggers into your brain, completely short-circuiting your ability to run. I hate it when that happens.

At the sound, the Evil One bolts with my thong. I stumble after him in warm pursuit. Hot pursuit went out the window when I got old, and now I am experiencing muscle cramps. He sees me and attempts to jump on the fence, trying to make a clean get away. Unfortunately for him, he can't make the leap with the thong. He drops the lavender scrap in the mud and scampers back to his tree.

I gingerly pick up my expensive, plague ridden thong and take it back into the house for disinfecting. Bugger. Now what I want to know is what was he planning on doing with it anyway?

Damn you squirrel.

THE BITCHY NEIGHBOR "THE COW"

Well, yesterday my friend Jason came over to help me finish the deck. I needed to attach one post and its cross piece and then place lattice all around the upper level. I went to Lowe's that afternoon, where I found out that the lattice comes in sheets of 8 x 4 and wouldn't fit into my Saturn sports car. So, I had them cut it into 20" tall sheets. This way I could stack them on top of each other and transport them easier. It was a perfect plan. I wouldn't need to borrow someone's huge pickup just to haul flimsy pieces of trellis home.

To be honest, it wasn't brain surgery and with the help of my electric saw (sans spider) and a Mikita drill we were almost done. I was looking forward to a nice, cold, frosty alcoholic reward when we heard the bellow. It seems The Cow heard the noise and needed to make her displeasure known. She leans her head out of her bedroom window to bitch at me yet again.

Yes, this is the same woman who came over to whine about my security light and the lights in my dining room waking her up. I had considered just turning the security light off if it would stop her bitching. But then I thought about it and got my brain back. I'm not doing anything wrong. I'm not breaking any laws. I own my home, she's a renter. Fuck her. Why should I tip toe around in the dark like a felon, in order not to disturb her? There are worse things I can think of to complain about besides my dining room lights. I could have loud music blasting, or piles of poo all over the place or a meth lab in my backyard, and she's going to complain about a light?

I get it now. When I didn't agree to shut off the security light, she decided to find something else to bitch about. She announces we need to stop our "construction" because it's past 7:00 pm. What? Construction? We have a power saw that made a grand total of eight cuts, a Makita power drill, an old school hammer and saw. We started work around 5:20 and are almost done. Again, I will ask the question, what construction are you talking about you Evil Cow?!

I tell her we should be finished in fifteen minutes. She just keeps ranting about us needing to stop since it's 7:00 pm and you can't do construction after 7:00 pm. I really don't think the City of Oakland would consider this construction. No heavy machinery. No permits or building plans. We are tacking lattice to a deck for fuck sake! She also blames the construction work from my kitchen remodel for sending mice and rats over to her place. Umm, I've never had any problem with rats or mice, and I told her so. If she has vermin, they aren't coming from my place. This is really getting frustrating. I can't even fix up my house so I can sell it without being judged by renters. This is the last straw.

I say she's welcome to call the police but by the time they arrive, we'll be done, not that we're doing anything wrong in the first place. She says she's just trying to be nice and won't call the police. Really? Then why threaten us with the cops in the first place? She says she will complain to the people she needs to complain to. Who would that be? God? Her landlord? I have news for her. Her landlord doesn't care. He's selling the place and also thinks she's a pain in the ass. My landlord? Oh right, that would be ME.

Frustrated that she "doesn't get her privacy" she gives up, goes back inside and we finish the one small section we have left. When we are done and the tools are all put away, the clock reads 7:10. That means she had to have been bitching at us to stop around 6:45.

Can you tell how ready I am for this to be over? I think someone needs to remind her of the saying, "The devil you know is better than the devil you don't." Who knows who will buy the house?

They may be playing death metal at all hours, or roasting a goat in the backyard or filling the house with twenty Samoans (I've seen it happen), and then she'll be begging for the days of just having a little saw noise and a light to complain about.

I wonder where I can rent twenty Samoans?

OPEN HOUSE #563

If you've never had the doors of your house flung open for the great-unwashed masses to pour through, you just haven't lived. When I was little, my mother used to take my sister and me to Open Houses on Sundays. It was an inexpensive way to get outside and see inside wonderful, fancy homes. Granted, the houses we saw were model homes and not actual people's houses but it was kind of the same thing.

I thought I would be fine with the concept of an Open House until it actually started happening. I became paranoid that strangers would go through my drawers, sniff my panties and judge my taste. The worst thing I could think of happening would be having some small items grow legs and walk off. My realtor assured me that since the house was on a lock box, any prospective buyers would be chaperoned at all times. It still made me nervous. Lock boxes made me nervous. The fact that a key to my front door was inside a box was disconcerting. I know the box is locked; hence the words lock box, but that didn't stop my paranoid brain from working overtime.

I also needed to be absent when buyers come by. I understood that. Prospective buyers do not like the owner lurking about while they figure out where they would put their TV or wonder why he or she bought that horrible couch. So, the Sunday Open Houses weren't that bad. I could leave for a few hours, go to the farmers market or take a drive to the beach and then return to an empty house. The showings I hate are the last minute ones. These are the phone calls you get from realtors asking if they can show your house, oh and they are right outside or just around the corner, and can they come right now?

Umm, not right now. What about the note that said to call the listing agent with an hour lead-time? Did they not read the entire listing? Apparently not. Now I have to run around and get the dirty dishes out of the sink, make sure the bed tray is artfully in place, at an angle, with a fresh rose in a bud vase and adjust the spa shelf that goes across the bathtub. I mean, everyone reads in the tub with a candle and some potpourri, don't they? Inevitably, the house smells like fish, since I was in the middle of cooking dinner.

I end up finishing the staging in ten minutes flat, call the realtor back and tell her to bring the potential buyers over. Then I race out to my car, fling the driver's seat flat down and hide like some kind of peeping felon. This way, I figure, I will be able to see when they leave and salvage the remains of my dinner. No one should have to lay in wait in their own car while strangers poke through their closet. It's just cruel.

This has been going on for months, and it's starting to make me rabid. I feel like one of those tiny rat dogs, shivering and shaking all the time. I'm getting neurotic. I would love to be rebellious, but I need to sell the house, and I'm afraid having a copy of The Satanic Bible on the coffee table would adversely affect my ability to close the deal.

I have discovered that the only thing standing between me and shaky rat dog syndrome is a glass of good wine. I figure everyone has to have a hobby, and I could do worse.

WHY ARE CATS ALWAYS JUDGING ME?

Thus is the nature of cats. Cats are judgmental, independent and vindictive. That's the reason people feel so passionately one way or the other about them. Piss off a cat, and they don't forget, they just save it up for later. They will wait a week and then piss in your shoe. They are completely unapologetic about their behavior.

I can just hear what is rolling around in their furry little heads. "Fine. You want to leave me for the weekend? Hope you like the present I left you on the stairs. You will discover it in the middle of the night as you are stumbling bleary-eyed down the hall to take a pee." Cats don't care. If they could open their own food they would have even less use for you.

I guess this is why I like cats with balls (not necessarily male you understand) instead of the needy ones. Then again, I don't like yippy rat dogs you have to carry around in a purse either. It's hard to have respect for a critter that would die if it fell off the couch. This is why I like cats with attitude, the ones who decide to teach you a lesson. They will lay by your face, so when you turn over in the middle of the night and crack open an eye - BAM! You get a whole face full of cat anus. That's always special.

Cats also purr and climb on your lap, or, as in the case of my demonic black basketball from Hell, demand to be picked up and placed on your lap, since the act of actually jumping is getting a little beneath his dignity and fat ass.

I know my niece and nephew were a little let down when they learned they had a "cat cousin" instead of a human one. I told them, "First, Auntie D isn't married. Second, Auntie D's eggs are stale. Third, you are all the kids that Auntie D wants to deal with for the rest of her life during holiday dinners, plus I can beat you and stick you in a closet." They seemed to think this was funny.

Well, it looks like the days of having a cat cousin are drawing to a close. My big, fat, gay cat is nineteen and in frail health. I decided it was time to take him in to the vet for The Big Sleep. I just couldn't stand the possibility of coming home from a vacation and finding out that he had died while I was away. I told the cat sitter if he croaked on her watch to wrap him in a towel, stick him in the freezer, leave a note that says "cat in freezer" and I'd deal with him later. It's bad enough having all this house stress, I don't want to sniff the air for tell-tale odors of death when I come home and have to deal with the disposal of his remains.

It was sad, but I've had Chauncy a long time. So after I got back from the vets, I went to my favorite Tiki bar and threw a wake. Yes, a wake for my cat! Come on, don't tell me you wouldn't pass up the opportunity to have flaming bowl drinks and hear the story about how my friend Dot peed on my cat.

See? Your ears are perking up right now. You are thinking, "Wait, did I hear that right? Your friend peed on your cat?" Yup, allow me to explain.

Male cats tend to spray to mark territory. This will still happen even if you get your cat fixed. Put two or more male cats in a house, and it's a regular pee-spectacular. Peeing on a cat's head, right after the spraying incident, is supposed to assert your dominance over the male cat and curb the behavior. The problem is being able to get the timing right. First, you have to catch the cat in the act. You can't just find cat pee, and then pee on the cat. The cat will have no idea why you are doing it. Second, you need to have a full bladder. So many times Dot had just used the bathroom and then Chauncy sprayed on a wall right in front of her. I think he was just doing it to piss her off, so to speak.

Well, one day the stars aligned. Chauncy peed on the front door; Dot had to go, so she grabbed the cat and got into the glass walled shower with him. The next thing I hear is a pitiful yowling coming from the bathroom. Then the door opens and my cat streaks out. His head and shoulders are wet. Yup, my roomie just peed on my cat.

You would think that's shocking enough, but it wasn't over yet. The cat makes a beeline for my room and jumps on my bed! So now I have Dot's pee on the bedspread. I grab the cat, toss him in my shower and turn on the water. That elicits a whole new set of renewed yowls. I proceed to wash the cat with shampoo. Baths are not Chauncy's favorite thing and since this was last minute, I don't have my normal protective gear.

When all is said and done, I have a wet, angry cat smelling like a garden of flowers that has just been pissed on. I have some scratches and a small bump where my head hit the cabinets after the newly shampooed cat launched himself out the door, using my body as a springboard.

Did it work? Actually, it did for a while. I seem to remember he didn't spray for a few months after that, but neither of us was willing to undergo another round of the pee fiasco to make this an ongoing lesson.

Well, now I am catless, jobless and stressed out. I keep telling myself it has to get better, but at the moment nothing seems right without my demonic black basketball from Hell.

MY ARCH NEMESIS THE SQUIRREL

So I have resigned myself to the fact that I have a Super Villain living in my back yard. Yes, an evil genius, a purveyor of mischief, murder and madcap mayhem. I am speaking about... The Squirrel.

Why do I fixate on this small, furry rodent? Why do I have fantasies of making a wee hat out of its hide? Why is it, when I see a squirrel road-kill carcass, I seriously debate the pros and cons of putting it in my lunch cooler, dismembering it, skinning it, taking pictures to prove it really happened and making the aforementioned hat even though this wasn't the squirrel in question and it was already squished by a car?

It's not because I'm disturbed. It's because squirrels hate me! I don't know why aside from the fact that gray squirrels seem to have a bad track record as far as their attitude goes. They are he bad boy squirrels of the U S of A. They have pretty much pushed out the indigenous red squirrel population in Britain. Yes, the nice red squirrel of Squirrel Nutkin/Beatrice Potter fame has been driven to near extinction by the pushy gray bully from across the pond. It reminds me of McDonalds, Wal-Mart and other American exports that spread with Borg-like intensity.

I tried to be nice to the belligerent varmint. I fed it chunky peanut butter, but that was my undoing. He is determined to get more of that squirrel crack and if he doesn't he will take my sanity. He has chattered at me, mocked me, chucked a wee lemon at my head, tossed small detritus at my window and, I believe, tried to relieve himself on my late, beloved cat Chauncy.

I'm not making this up. My cat was in the backyard, just sitting on that ugly cement pad, minding his own business. All of a sudden, I saw the squirrel run into the tree, hang his butt over a branch right above my cat's head and take aim. I swear to God! He would adjust, moving back and forth to get right over Chauncy's head. Chauncy was old and didn't see him, but there was no way I was going to let that rodent piddle or drop a mookie stick on my baby's head. So I yelled at the squirrel and off he ran, foiled again.

Bugger.

So now my cat is dead. I'm losing my mind, and all I have to fixate on is the squirrel. I think I'm going to start constructing a devious machine of destruction, a contraption worthy of The Riddler or The Penguin. Something an arch-villain would construct when they captured Batman.

Although, even as a child, I wondered why the villains didn't just shoot Batman and the Boy Wonder in the head instead of tying them up in those bondage contraptions which just give them time to escape? Will it be the same with the squirrel, or maybe I should just pop a cap in the little bugger's ass?

I suppose only time will tell.

WALL STREET IS IN FREEFALL BUT RABBITS WILL ALWAYS BE CRAZIER

Offers on my house have stalled. Okay, let's be honest, there weren't any offers. There was interest, lots of interest, but no offers. My house is small and only has one bedroom, so that cuts down the pool of people who would be interested in buying it. It was priced according to market value, but we still lowered the price and relisted it. A few times it looked like an offer was going to come in, then Wall Street hit freefall and everything went to Hell in a hand basket. That hand basket is getting pretty familiar and way too crowded lately.

All those potential buyers who were waiting for the market to drop, are now too scared to buy. They think prices will go even lower. The banks have practically stopped lending money. People figure if they wait long enough they could pick up a house at a foreclosure auction for a deep discount. I watched all my hopes of starting over go up in smoke. Let me make one thing clear, that smoke was made up of all the money a handful of entitled asshats was currently burning through.

So, once it hit me that selling my house has hit the skids, I decided to start hauling my things up from the basement and back into the house. I wanted my pictures back, I wanted my books and I wanted my life to have some kind of normalcy again, at least for the short-term. A friend of mine brought her pet bunny over to "cheer me up." It was akin to bringing the Killer Rabbit from "Monty Python and the Holy Grail" 'round for tea.

Everyone thinks bunnies are these cute, fluffy little creatures. Small, docile little dollops of creamy petable love. Let me tell you something. Bunnies can be evil. I know, I know, first the squirrels, now the bunnies. I can hear the comments now. "What's wrong with you? Did Bugs Bunny leave a present in your breakfast cereal as a child?" Not exactly, it just seems to me that when I look back though my life, I've always been on the wrong side of a rabbit.

When I was little, my Dad got my sister and me rabbits for Easter. My sister was envious that I got the white bunny that looked like the Easter Rabbit. Meanwhile, I wanted her black and white rabbit. We didn't figure that out until much later. I learned that rabbits pooped a great deal. They were large and really not that affectionate. Face it, they aren't dogs.

The Effect of Gamma Rays on Man-in-the-Moon Marigolds. If you are familiar with the play, you know that a rabbit plays a major thematic part in the show. In fact, I got to bring the body of the dead rabbit out at the end (really a sneaker wrapped in a towel) and drop it on the stage. It made a sickening thud. It was great. Didn't mean to spoil the end of the play for you, but yes, the rabbit dies. The rabbit is murdered, actually. It's a great play, though not because of rabbit murder.

Anyway, we borrowed a small dwarf Dutch bunny from the local pet store for the show. We promptly named him Moon Unit. The bunny was on a leash the entire time he was on stage, tethered to a chair. We never had a problem with him. That was until Pat was cast in the show. Pat was our local lesbian/male cross dresser. She was playing the part of the science teacher ala Indiana Jones. One night Pat just freaked out. Who knows what goes through Pat's mind when she is under stress and missing the latest drill bit convention. I was backstage, waiting for my cue, when Pat starts running around yelling, "The rabbit's going flat! The rabbit's going flat!"

"Huh?"

Going flat? He looked perfectly three dimensional to me. Then without warning, she runs on stage, grabs the rabbit and runs off. Wow – a run-by rabbit napping, in front of a live audience, by the crazy cross-dressing science teacher. How do you work that into the show? My fellow actors just chose to ignore the fact that Mr. Science Teacher ran into their living room, stole their daughters' rabbit and ran out again, all the while ranting about the rabbit "going flat."

I have no idea what the audience thought, but if mind control has any basis in reality, all of us intently thinking, "These are not the droids you're looking for" may have had some effect on the audience. At least no one mentioned the unfortunate incident again.

Later in life, my friends decided to get me a little bunny, a cute little bunny, as a pet. The rodent bit me. To be fair, I will have to say I deserved it. I was having a small case of puppy envy and thought I could train the bunny to behave more like a dog. I was trying to stuff it into a cat harness at the time so I could take it for a walk or a drag as the case may be. The bunny didn't react well to this. It squirmed, it kicked its feet and then it sunk its rather sharp tooth into my finger.

I realize I didn't go to medical school, but I know what happens when you don't clean bites out thoroughly. In fact, I know first hand because I didn't clean the bunny bite out thoroughly enough and my finger became majorly infected. I'm talking horror movie stuff here. It swelled and it hurt so bad I couldn't even touch it lightly without excruciating pain. I had no insurance, so I went to the local barber surgeon AKA our Dungeon Master's boyfriend. (Yes, we played D&D, don't judge me!) I had him slice open the bite with an Exacto knife and we re-cleaned it thoroughly. I was biting on something as I recall. A bullet, a towel, someone's arm – I can't remember. You see? This is what happens when people don't have health care! They are forced to go to some guy on a corner armed with a bottle of vodka and an Exacto knife.

I do remember that the bunny was soon sent packing, and I still have the scar on my finger where he bit me. They are fluffy little packages of cute, I'll give you that, but they can be evil and crazy mean. A little like Lindsay Lohan on a bender of diet pills and crack cocaine – Allegedly!

I guess I would be a little crazy mean as well if my purpose in life was to be dinner.

OUR LADY OF PERPETUAL PENANCE

Yesterday I was walking home past the Church of the Great Glass Cooter and I saw something very disturbing. I know, just the fact that I have to walk by that Stalinist-styled bunker of a church is disturbing, but even more so was the fleet of super stretch limos pulling up in front.

The limos were off-loading priests, nuns in full and half-habits and various collared clergy. Yes, it was the million-dollar Papist parade. Umm, I was a little confused. Why did they need all the limos? It seems Our Lady of Perpetual Indulgence is having a gala of sorts. I'm convinced they invited me, but my invitation obviously was lost in the mail. I slowed down to watch the line of limos pulling up to the curb to deposit their collared passengers on a red carpet, a sight worthy of the Oscars.

As I watched, something started to bother me. Why this outpouring of gilt for a religious event? Here's an idea: instead of renting P. Diddy's whole stable of "about town transport," how about renting a few town cars or a station wagon (do they even make those anymore) or a van? If they had to have limos, why did they have to be super stretch? Visions of drunken orgies on plush seats with overhead neon track lighting and Nuns Gone Wild being filmed in the cavernous interior, dance in my head. Flashes of Sister Mary Margaret, popping out of the sky roof, tits to the wind with a bottle of bubbly in her hand, hooting, "Bride of Christ My Ass!" run through my head faster than a jack rabbit on a date.

I'm sure these old, dried-up, Sunday school women are perfect handmaidens in waiting to my fiancé; who insists he just has them around to wash his donkey when it gets dirty. But the whole thing seems a bit extravagant to me. The Big JC agrees and then complains that he's hungry. I remind him I still need to go to the store, I am sick of fish, but if he'll take care of the wine and the bread I can whip up some steaks. Judas is coming over to play Rock Band with us. I'm making him play drums because I suck at them. I figure, since he keeps bragging about how he's good at everything, he can play the drum solo by The Who on Expert mode. He's always saying he knows what's best for everyone. Yeah, how did that work out for you last time? But I digress...

It seems the Cathedral is being dedicated this weekend, which involves digging up the first bishop of the original Oakland church and reinterring him in the cement mausoleum under the holy glass cootch. Great. So, the place in overrun by TV vans and cameras, reception tables and Jesuits with radios and ear pieces (that should surprise no one). Security barriers and limos and nuns and punch. It sounds like a party to me.

I was sorely tempted to take a picture of said nuns in the super stretch limo but was afraid the Jesuits would beat the crap out of me, smash my camera and then excommunicate me. So I walked on, still wondering how much those limos cost and wouldn't a nice homey community event have been nicer? They could have raised money and celebrated at the same time with a lemonade stand. Everyone likes a little kid selling lemonade. It would be innocent and wholesome and full of lost family values. Oh yeah, I forgot about the problem the church has with little kids.

Instead, I just head home. While crossing the street, I am almost run down in the crosswalk by an 80-year-old Asian granny who can barely see over the wheel. That is the other bane of my existence. 80-year-old Asian grannies. They are the only ones who have ever tried to send me to the next world via vehicular manslaughter.

They must be in league with the Catholics.

ONCE YOU HIT BOTTOM, YOU BOUNCE!

What do you do when your options have run out, the world of government cheese is looming and creditors are calling fifty times a day? You go to an attorney. After long hours of sleepless nights, I have decided to swallow my pride and declare bankruptcy. It sucks, but right now it's the only way out of the ever-increasing suck hole that is becoming my life, and I mean this in a quicksand way, not some gross porn star way.

How do you go about finding a bankruptcy attorney? Well, there are tons of infomercials on the TV (usually during the Jerry Springer show because that's what the out of work losers are watching), or you can just stick your finger in the phone book and pick one. I was really tempted by some of the ambulance chasing infomercials, but in the end I went with an attorney a friend recommended.

I have a bit of experience with lawyers. My father was one. I know what a lawyer's office is supposed to look like and how it's supposed to be run. I guess this guy didn't get the memo. His receptionist is lucky to have a third grade education judging by her phone manner, how she greeted clients and her total lack of knowledge about anything at all. I have no idea why she has a job and I don't. Life just isn't fair.

This whole experience is worse than going to the dentist and buying condoms at the drug store when you were sixteen combined. I think it's the label of shame involved. Those of us who were brought up with Ovaltine, Hawaii 5-0 and a work ethic were taught to pay our debts and not be a burden to society. There was always an unspoken mantra of, "Thou Shalt Not Go On The Dole!" in the air. However, I have learned there are times when you just do what you need to do in order to get back on your feet.

I finally meet with my attorney, pay my retainer and hear about what I need to do in order to file for bankruptcy. Is there an upside to this whole painful experience? Actually, yes. I won't have to worry about paying the mortgage on the house anymore. The house will go back to the bank, I will not owe anything on it and my creditors will stop camping out on my sidewalk, eating bologna sandwiches and glaring at me. I highly recommend this when all else fails. Declaring bankruptcy, not eating bologna sandwiches in front of people's houses.

I feel like a giant weight has been lifted from my shoulders. I can finally sleep at night, my creditors are prohibited from calling me and if they do there is something satisfying in telling them to "talk to my attorney."

IRONS ARE HOT: A LESSON IN THE OBVIOUS

My ironing board pops out of the wall. How's that for a random declaration? This feature was considered to be a nice "built-in" device when my house was constructed in the 1920's. The only issue I have with it is the location of said ironing board. It's in the kitchen. You open this long door and lo and behold, there is a wooden ironing board all folded up into the wall, ready to be used. The fact that it's been hanging out there for the past eighty years with the cover moldering is a little freaky I must admit. I always intended on removing the board, making wee shelves and turning that little recessed area into a spice rack. I just never got around to doing it.

My kitchen is really narrow, so having the ironing board there requires a bit of juggling on my part. First, I have to move my fridge over towards the back door. I can either open the ironing board cupboard far enough to get the board out, or I can open the back door. I can't do both. My refrigerator isn't huge, but when this house was built, most people got by using ice boxes and hanging their food up in trees during the winter. I guess the squirrel population explosion hadn't occurred yet.

Once the board is down, it nearly spans the entire area between the wall and the counter, and I can't walk around it. There is only a foot of clearance between the end of the board and the edge of the counter. Don't I have a normal metal ironing board? Sure I do. It's in the basement. I really don't want to haul things down to the basement to iron them nor do I want to cart the board into the house every time I need to iron something. Ironing isn't one of my favorite things. It's not fun like playing with puppies, drinking Irish Car Bombs or building a bridge to Japan.

Even though I avoid ironing when at all possible, I do know how to do it. I know how to iron sleeves. I know you don't lay a hot iron flat down on its face especially if your clothes are underneath it at the time. That leads to iron-shaped scorch marks and possible fires. I realize that irons are hot, especially if you set them to the highest setting which is either Linen or Fuck That's Hot.

So, the other day I needed to iron a costume piece. Everything was fine. I was wide awake and sober. I must have bumped the ironing board because the iron started to fall. Instead of just letting it fall, I reached out and grabbed it. I like to think it was my cat-like reflexes that leapt into action, unbidden, when they saw a task. I really wish my reflexes would have consulted with my brain first because reaching out and grabbing a hot iron by any part other than the handle is what we call "a bad idea."

Yes, I burned my hand. It was bad. It wasn't as bad as getting branded. There was no searing flesh but there was yelling, cursing and quickly dropping the offending iron. My brain picked that time to send the memo to my cat-like reflexes that irons are hot and just because something is falling doesn't mean you always have to catch it. See? The iron fell anyway but this time you have a bad burn to show for your over eager behavior.

I immediately run my hand under the faucet but can see the welt rising on my palm. Great. I have no first-aid kit in the house. It's not that I don't have one but it's in my dressing room at the theatre as I'm in the middle of a show. So I don't have any aloe vera gel to help with the blisters and welts this second degree burn has caused. I must admit, I freaked out.

Ruthie is always available for riding to my rescue with her abundance of medical supplies. I have a feeling she stock piles in case of nuclear winter or impromptu Red Cross drill. I give her a call, whine about my burned hand, my idiot cat-like reflexes and then whined some more for good measure. It's amazing how I can go from "strong woman" to "whiny bitch" in two point three seconds when faced with a situation outside of my comfort zone.

I must say, it wasn't so much the pain factor, it was the fact that I was in a show and needed the use of my hand that weekend that scared me most. As I sat with my hand in a bowl of ice water, I had time to realistically assess my situation and decide how to handle this. I thought clear communication would be the best answer. How wrong I was.

Why are men so clueless? The weekend comes around, and I tell everyone in the cast that I burned my hand and not to touch it or grab it. I figured those instructions were pretty clear. So what did the majority of the men do? Grab my hand. They didn't do it to be mean, they were just clueless. When I talk, am I like the teacher in the Charlie Brown specials who just sounds like "whah whah, whah whah whah" or do men just see boobs and then cease to assimilate any other data? If so, how do they function in business? Is this why some men don't want to work with women? Because once distracted by boobs, their brains would seize and nothing would get done. I have no idea.

Honestly, women aren't like that. We don't spend our time staring at men's crotches. Well, not unless it's really obvious and then it's just like a train wreck. So glaringly freakish you are unable to avert your eyes. The only threat left to me is promising to punch the offending men in the junk if they grab my hand again. Perhaps the pain factor will make them pay attention to what I'm saying.

I can only hope.

IF OTHER ANIMALS CAN EAT THEIR YOUNG, WHY CAN'T WE?

As I was surfing the 563 channels of total crap that passes itself off for television programming these days, I came upon a nature show which got me thinking about how short life really is. I sat around, getting more depressed and really wishing I had a small puppy I could play with. Barring puppies, I decided to contemplate the serious epidemic of cannibalism among hamsters and what we can learn from them.

Word on the street has it that hamsters sometimes eat their young. It tends to be the females that do this though the males have been known to chow down on their offspring as well. I just love the fact that one website I found states, "If this happens to you, here are some factors you may have done that may (or may not) have caused it."

Wow, talk about a guilt trip! It's all your fault that your hamster ate her babies, you bad monkey! Do we really need more reasons to feel bad about ourselves? Another hamster website says, "The reason why mothers eat their babies is that they feel that the babies will not live long, so instead of prolonging their suffering, they eat them."

Umm, I think this doof is projecting his own human experiences on this rodent. I really don't think "web guy" has a PhD in hamster biology and come on – It's a hamster! It has a brain the size of a Tic Tac! Do you really think it's trying to save its offspring from suffering because, with its Super Hamster Brain Power, it can tell

173

its life is short? Of course it's short! It's a hamster and that little baby hamster looks kinda tasty.

Now what do the scientists say? They say this eating one's offspring behavior can be caused by:
1. Stress
2. Someone touched them and got monkey smell on them
3. The offspring were runty or deformed
4. The offspring were viewed as a perceived threat
5. The mother needed the protein
6. The mother was freaked out by the birth

The truth is, the scientists don't really know why hamsters eat their spawn. These are just theories, or as we like to say, "wild ass guesses which may or may not be correct." Now, what I want to know is, can we parallel the reproductive oddities of a hamster with humans? I mean, I think there are times when it should be justifiable for mothers to eat their young. So, let's go down the hamster list and see how it adds up.

1. Stress: Okay, mothers have that in spades. They are always stressed, sleep deprived and I've heard that having a baby drains your brain functions and makes you stupid. I can't even count the number of times various female friends have claimed "baby brain" as an excuse for shoes on the wrong feet, putting keys in the fridge or infanticide.

2. You touched them and got monkey smell on them: Fine, you touch the baby all the time but the thing here is that something alien and foreign touched the baby, making it smell funny and causing the mother to reject it. I think babies have funny smells down pat and since everyone on the planet wants to touch your baby – Bingo! Perfect defense. Someone got some weird smell on it, it didn't smell like mine anymore, so I ate it.

3. They were runty or deformed: I think you can make the argument that just because you were born small or funny looking, doesn't mean you will stay that way. But why take that chance? There is ketchup in the cupboard.

4. Viewed as a perceived threat: This is an easy one. So many modern mothers are self-absorbed, trend following, bags of hair who would see a wee little baby as a threat to the attention that should be on her. We all know that babies suck up all the attention in a room and that is threatening.

5. Needed the protein: Another easy one. "Your Honor, I was on the Atkins diet and all the hospital had to eat was carbs."

6. Freaked out by the birth: Yeah, that's a given. How many kids claim they didn't even know they were pregnant until they gave birth in a bathroom stall, chucked the baby in the bin and then went back to the Prom. We know that happens. I've seen multiple news stories and shows on Dr. Phil.

So this bears the question. Are we better than hamsters? Of course we are! We have opposable thumbs, brains bigger than Tic Tacs and, for the most part, love and want our children. However, it's always good to have a fall-back position. Just think, the next time your kid gives you grief, all you have to do is point to the hamster and then the ketchup bottle.

He'll get the point.

MANLY, GAY CUCUMBER DRINKS

Well I finished a three-month job assignment and I can't think of anything that says "welcome back to the rat race" more than a frosty tiki drink. So I packed up my trusty Moleskine, a nice gel pen, all the spare change I could scrounge from the sofa and headed over to Forbidden Island. All the way to Alameda, that flaming bowl drink was calling my name. No really, I heard it. It started out with a seductive whisper and ended up shrieking like a demented three-year old hopped up on sugar and crack. Let me tell you, by the time I landed at "Tiki Central", I needed that drink more than ever.

I've been working on an article for a magazine for the past week and figured there was no reason why I couldn't mix writing with drinking. It made sense to me though I can't picture Papa Hemmingway with a frosty island drink festooned with paper umbrellas and a plastic monkey. I decided to sit at the bar this time, eschewing the tables in favor of something a little closer to the action and to the bartender.

On my left I noticed two guys sitting next to me. They each had a mug with a whole cucumber stuck in it. One guy's cucumber was peeled and the other cucumber was only half shaved. Both were cut (tops cut off and the inside hollowed out). They were covered in cling film and stuck out like spaghetti at Thanksgiving dinner.

Whoa. I need to stop the article writing now and switch to making notes. Strange things often happen in a bar but this bit of weirdness was outside the norm. I ask the guys about their cucumbers, why they brought their own cucumbers into the bar and wouldn't it have been more festive if they had carved their cucumbers? They said they did, pointing to the gutted veggies. That is so not what I meant. Why are guys so fuckin' clueless? And no, I didn't turn to them and say, "You should have carved those cucumbers to look like a penis, you know - a big COCK - because it's a cucumber! And it's standing upright in a glass!" No, I didn't say that. I shouldn't have to. The joke was too obvious but not for the straight guys. The gays would have gotten it. In fact, they would have brought in more festive cucumbers, and they wouldn't have been half shaved.

Anyway, they tell me that they come to the Tiki bar every Tuesday and the bartender keeps a book of theirs behind the bar that lists various Tiki drinks in alphabetical order. They are drinking their way through the book and today they are on "C" the "C" drink calls for a cucumber. You pour the drink into the cucumber, suck the drink through a straw inserted into the hollowed out cuke and then nibble the cucumber as you drain your drink. Sounds pretty gay to me. Boys, are you sure you didn't buy that book in the Castro?

I continue to observe these guys. Yes, they were totally straight. They sucked on their straws, they talked about basketball, they looked at the next drink in the book and looked slightly uncomfortable. I just had to chime in again.

"Hey guys, aren't you supposed to be eating those cucumbers?" They look at me. "I'm just sayin'. You said it was part of the rules." They look at me again and then say, "Yeah, I guess you're right," and start making half-hearted nibbles into their respective cucumbers. Their slightly uncomfortable air gave way to full out panic. It was almost like they were ten years old again, back in their bedrooms, petrified that their Mom would walk in on them masturbating to a picture of Farrah Fawcett .

The guy with the half shaved cucumber is having trouble. I decide to be helpful Hannah yet again. "You know, if you shaved that completely like your friend, it would be easier to eat. It's kind of bitter that way." I didn't add, "Especially when you smoke," because that would be rude, they would be clueless and I would think they were dumber than they currently are. I go back to drinking my frosty beverage and writing my article.

I tried to ponder the meaning of cucumbers, life and everything. It was just making my brain hurt. Besides, the guys at the bar were taking their nibbled cucumbers and heading out. I decided to pack it in, take my article home and get it sorted out later. After all, tomorrow is another day and who could write a historical piece on Tudor monarchs after watching the cucumber show? I know I can't.

My brain needs a rest.

THE GIANT, BELLOWING COW FROM ACTON, OHIO RIDES AGAIN

As you know, I have this neighbor who has a mouth as big as Texas, an ass as wide as Russia and an attitude as nasty as Osama Bin Laden stuck in a sweltering desert cave with one hundred other men and no shower. We've been having a running battle, usually over my electricity use.

Now it seems, if I have a guest over, and I happen to have the lights on in the dining room past 10pm she gets all annoyed. She claims the lights shine in her bedroom window (which overlooks my backyard) as bright as the sun, and she can't sleep even with blinds and a curtain and a sleep mask. I think her head is so big that the mask keeps sliding up. Who knows?

What I do know is when I was getting ready to go to bed last night. I notice something odd. It's around one or two in the morning and I'm turning off the lights when I notice there's a slow flashing strobe coming in through my dining room window.

What the Hell?

Yeah, she's taken a road safety light with a flasher, stuck it in her living room window (below my dining room window) and set it to flash. O Kay. Umm, my bedroom is behind the dining room, so unless that flasher is filled with kryptonite and some secret radioactive material; it can't get through a door/wall to bother me.

179

I just can't believe this latest stunt was supposed to piss me off. Whatever. The last time she threatened to call the cops I told her to go ahead. Honestly, I wasn't breaking the law, and my boyfriend is a lieutenant at the local precinct. I'm sure he would love to have a talk with her about filing false police reports against his girlfriend.

Fine, I don't have a boyfriend who is a policeman. In fact, I don't have a boyfriend. I think it would be really cool to have a cop as a boyfriend, especially one with a pension. The point is, she doesn't know I don't have a cop boyfriend. I have so many pretend "boyfriends" you wouldn't believe. Honestly!

The other reason for the boyfriend ruse is the street parking. If you show up to my house after 7pm, there is nowhere to park unless you want to leave your car on the sidewalk, which I don't advise. My driveway is very short and has a steep drop from the sidewalk to the drive itself. Basically it was designed for a Model T Ford. Those cars have a ton of clearance. Most of our cars are lower to the ground so unless you are driving an SUV, if you try to park in my driveway, your undercarriage will hit the pavement.

So, when I park in front of my house, I position my car so there is enough room for my guest to park blocking my driveway. While it is illegal to block other people's drives, you can block your own. However, there are tons of clueless people who seem to think that a space in front of a person's driveway is fair game. All they see is a glowing invitation to park their huge metal ass there themselves. Too many times I have to lean out the window, screaming like a demented fish wife, yelling at people to move their car from in front of my driveway.

To be fair, seven out of ten people have the decency to look abashed and drive off. Two out of ten try the, "I was just stopping for a little while" excuse while that one asshat tries to argue with me. If they get pissy, I pull the "instant boyfriend card" out of my pocket. I tell them that my boyfriend/husband is on his way home and if he doesn't get to park his car in his driveway there will be a heap of hurt going down. These imaginary guys are cops, firefighters, marines, special forces, CIA operatives, the usual.

Although it kinda blows the illusion when a carload of them show up in drag, but that's another story.

THERE IS A DEAD X-MAN IN SPLASH POO MANSION

Well, on the advice of my attorney, I have stopped paying my mortgage. I am just going to stay in the house until I get tossed out by the bank. I really have no other choice. It was the only thing I could do in order to stay afloat. I feel a little weird squatting in the house I so proudly purchased just four years ago. I try not to think about losing the job I loved, losing the life I had and now losing my house. At least I have a roof over my head and good friends. Oh yes, I should count my blessings for the wonderful neighbors I have as well. Then I think about Splash Poo Mansion and the Unhappy Cow, and I have an urge to raid the liquor cabinet.

I have to admit I've kept an eye out for more strobe attacks from the Unhappy Cow. It's been three weeks and there's been nothing. Either she's figured out this tactic doesn't work, or she is lulling me into a false sense of security. Either way, I've had more disturbing things to worry about. The slide of the economy into another Depression? No, it's worse. I know, what could be worse than lines for government cheese? I'll tell you.

Last night I was getting ready to go to bed. I walked over to my bedroom window, overlooking the living room of Splash Poo Mansion, and saw the most disturbing sight ever. Okay it was the frackin' scariest thing I've seen in quite some time. It was definitely scarier than seeing Mr. and Mrs. Splash Poo Mansion naked, and that is pretty damn scary.

Sitting in the middle of the trash-strewn room was a dead X-Man. Really! I think it was that Night Crawler, Hungarian circus guy. I just caught a glimpse, and it scared me so bad that I shut the curtains and tried to pretend it wasn't there. I've found pretending something doesn't exist works for lots of things like ex-boyfriends, spiders, and cleaning the toilet. I tried, but I just couldn't get the picture out of my head. What if Mr. and Mrs. Splash Poo Mansion had actually popped an X-Man?

I thought, at first, maybe I was seeing things. Perhaps it was just a pile of boxes and a strange shadow. I screwed up my courage and took another peek through the curtains. It was dark, the light was on in their living room and their whole house was covered in shit as usual.

Now, I've seen their crap piles before, but across from the window, in the center of their dining room was a body. Yup, a body! It was about the size of an eight to ten year old child. The skin was a nasty black/blue/grey (like the guy in X-Men). Its eyes were open and staring, and it had a grimace on its face. It was as if someone had made a nasty voodoo doll out of human skin, mummified it, buried it, dug it up and then sat it in the living room facing my window as a happy conversation piece.

IT FREAKED ME OUT! Very little freaks me out. Snakes? Nope. Rats and mice? Nada. Roaches? Don't like them, but they don't make me woogy. Dead People? Not so much, aside from the fact that the dead can be kinda bossy. The paranormal is normal for me. No big freak factor there except I really wish the ADD dead person living in my closet would stop it already with the watching TV in the middle of the night because it's starting to piss me off.

So, not a lot of things freak me out. Well, there are spiders. Large spiders. They freak me out, but this was worse. Much worse. George Romero has got nothing on whatever is sitting in that shit-filled room right now peering into my bedroom. I closed the curtains to block my view. I decided to investigate in the morning, if I could find my balls. I think they used to belong to one of my exes and the last time I saw them I think they were in a drawer.

Either a drawer or a purse. Anyway, this thing is scary, really! Especially since it was dark and I was alone and the squirrel is still lurking outside somewhere...

As I lay in bed, I started thinking. Maybe I should knock on their door and ask, "Ummm, dead X-Man? What the hell?" At least it's never boring over here. I figured that wouldn't work. They would either deny it or they would kill me too. So, I tried to think of pleasant things like puppies and fois gras and Disneyland.

Morning dawns a mite too early for my taste and I'm off to a temp job. When I got home, I steeled myself for another peek. I admit I was a bit nervous about peering into zombieland to check out whether or not the scary whatever-it-is would continue to stare at me. Once the sun set and the lights in Splash Poo Mansion came on, I wandered over to the window to play Peeping Tom CSI. I peeped though the curtain. I saw that the crap in the room had been joined by three large, empty cardboard boxes. I got a ladder and stood on it (with the pantomime of fiddling with my curtain rods) in order to peer over the box-shit clutter. I saw something move, but it was just a cat. The "dead X-Man" was nowhere to be found.

The next day I discovered that the chair the scary cadaver was sitting in was now on the curb. It was missing an arm and didn't appear to be stained with any fluid. I didn't have any luminol to check for blood trace. I really should just let this whole obsession go.

I wondered if I should call Oakland's Finest and tell them my dead X-Man story. That idea lasted until later in the afternoon. I saw the Mistress of Splash Poo Mansion, sitting at the side of the road. She was either catching her breath after her walk or waiting for the police.

I contemplated asking her, "So? I thought I saw a dead X-Man in your dining room. What was it?" but if I had a dead X-Man in my dining room and someone asked me about it I would say, "Nothing," or "It's a prop" or "My demonic imp from the fires of Hell was taking a breather."

The police think I'm crazy anyway, what with the Unhappy Cow neighbor and the people blocking my driveway and my various "boyfriends" that the cow hates. I'll just keep an eye out and the camera ready. I mean, calling Oakland PD and telling them I saw a dead X-Man is not probable cause.

They would probably lock me up for wasting their time and I can't say I would blame them.

OFF TO STATELY WAYNE MANOR

My temp job ended a week ago, and I'm back on the dole. The whole thing is just too depressing to even contemplate for any length of time. This only means one thing. Road Trip! I need to escape to the land of sun, surf and poison water. Yes, Los Angeles, the City of Angels, is where I go when I want to hide and lick my wounds. I'm staying with my good friends Roxy and Rex at their home, Stately Wayne Manor, for a few days. I'm going to house sit while they jet off to Wyoming.

What's in Wyoming? I think they're going to hang out with Robert Redford at his ski lodge. Naw, they don't know Robert Redford, and I have no idea whether he even has a ski lodge. Knowing the Sundance Kid, probably not, but it sounded much more glamorous and exotic that way. Actually they're renting a cabin with friends and drinking.

So here I am. Saturday morning, butt crack of dawn, at the Oakland Airport - I hate life. Whoever invented early mornings and stupid shuttle drivers needs a boot in the junk.. I booked a shuttle to drop me at the airport. I called on Thursday, got a quote and booked the trip. They called back on Friday night to confirm. Sounds great so far, right? Well it wasn't.

The night before was so hella hot I couldn't sleep. I was up at 4:15am, packing, watching a movie, making myself some eggs – normal stuff. 11:00am arrives and no shuttle. I get my phone out of my computer bag to check the time and find two messages. It was A__ whom I spoke with earlier. I'm thinking, due to his heavy accent, that he obviously was not born in this country. His message says that he's on the freeway, calling to confirm and since I'm not picking up the phone, he's going back and I can find my own way to the airport. What the fuck?!

I call him back. I don't raise my voice. I don't call him names, or say that I think his country of origin would look lovely as a sea of glass. I don't do any of those things. Am I thinking it? Yeah, I'm mad, but I am calm as he screams at me in a mixture of What-the-Fuckistan and broken English. I tell him to stop screaming at me. It's rude, and I can't stop myself from asking him, "Why on God's green earth is this happening when I confirmed with you last night? I was packing this morning, the phone was not on me. If my picking up the phone when you were on your way was a requirement, why didn't you let me know last night when we spoke?" He just screams some more in his unintelligible tongue and hangs up on me!

OK, by now I really wish fleas would infest not only his armpits but those of his entire family while they're at it. This is not how you do business. Perhaps in his country screaming is the norm, and maybe in his country I would have to wear a full body condom, but I'm here, not there.

So I get into my car, drive to Airpark and drop off my car. I am flying Jet Blue but hike over to the new terminal first so I can pick up a Chinese Chicken Salad at California Pizza Kitchen. This is my go-to snack of choice for food on the plane since I have eaten so many Southwest peanuts in my life, I half expect to grow a trunk. I make a beeline to the refrigerator case and they are all out of Chinese Chicken Salad. I am in heels! High heels! I'm not used to tottering all over Hell and gone in heels and this extra trip doesn't do my feet any favors. Thank the Gods for the Evil Entity known as Starbucks. I get a grande, non-fat, no water, chai tea latte and head all the way back to Terminal One so I can collapse into one of their "oh so comfortable" airport chairs.

They are renovating Terminal One, which is a good thing, but there isn't much in the way of good food to be found, which is not a good thing. I've also noticed that the fire sprinklers don't work. I guess in the event of a "carbon condition" we can all piss on the fire. You gotta love Oakland!

I sit down, pull out the laptop and try to get some work done. After half an hour I notice there's no airplane outside. Well, I go up to the little podium and notice the next surprise. It seems the Gods haven't given me enough grief already.My flight is delayed half an hour. Of course it is.

I just hope the car service in Long Beach figures that out. I must say, I love car services, mainly because I so love seeing my name on a sign. I will just assume that once we are in the air things will improve. Unfortunately they don't.

First, Jet Blue is now charging $1 for the cheesy headsets. I don't care because I have my iPod ear buds but still. It just seems all airlines do is raise prices and cut services. Pretty soon they will be charging you to use the toilet!

Second, they don't even have Terra Blue potato chips. I mean, this is their signature snack. How can this happen? I was devastated. We all know it's a cost cutting measure. Instead of offering a selection of six items, they have only two and rotate the choices. I was a sad, sad panda. They should always have the blue chips. I think the flight attendant felt sorry for me and my sad panda face. She found me a bag of blue chips that was probably squirreled away for the pilot. I didn't care. I was a happy camper.

Once we landed in Long Beach, I felt like running down the air stairs in a fit of glee. I was nearly at Stately Wayne Manor! I got off the plane and entered the main shoebox. I don't really consider it a terminal. It's a temporary building, a wee square box. A terminal is a shining corridor of glass, Starbucks kiosks and quiet desperation. This shoebox is not only small but it smells like feet. Phew. Bad, nasty cheese feet. Great.

I try to walk, not think of the cheese smell and keep my eye on the exit doors when I received a shock. I don't even know how to describe this but I am going to try. Picture a skinny, beanpole guy. 6 feet tall, 110 pounds, long brown hair, wire rim glasses, tank top and white pants. The pants are white denim but they have large, and I am talking 8" long, red ladybugs all over them. Ladybugs! I shit you not. I can't even call these gay pants because no self-respecting gay man would wear these. No drag queen worth her stilettos would wear these. No straight man worth his tenuous sexuality would wear these. I am shocked. My mouth really does drop open.

Mr. Ladybug doesn't set off my gaydar. He doesn't give off the straight vibe either. I get it. He's an alien. Ooo, better yet, he's a wizard from the Harry Potter universe. You know, the ones who don't know how to dress like Muggles but think they do. This is a prime example! I'm in shock. I just stare. I can't help it, it's like a train wreck. You just can't turn away from the ladybug pants. He turns and sees me gaping at him like a carp tossed out of the Koi pond. He says, "Oh, you mean these aren't cool? Guess I'll have to take them back now." I blink, nod and head for the doors.

I exit the wee terminal, hurry out to baggage claim and see... nothing. There is no guy with a sign. The guy from the car service is usually waiting patiently with a sign that has my name on it. No sign is on the horizon. I look around, walk to the curb. No guy. Great. My sad panda face is starting to re-emerge.

I call the car service. "Umm, where is my car? I don't see my driver." They tell me he's there. I say he must have activated his cloaking device because there are five people here and I don't see my driver. I don't see anyone with a sign. I see two scary cougars in spandex, a teen playing a game on his handheld and a college age couple making out. I doubt any of them are my driver. I've had a bad day and I just want my car.

I describe myself to the operator hoping that will help my invisible driver find me. I am in fear of being stranded in Long Beach with no way to Stately Wayne Manor. I haven't eaten anything but the contraband blue chips since 5am. It's hot, I'm cranky and my life looks bleak. Just when I thought I would have to dig through the trash MacGyver style and make transportation from a trash can, rubber bands, a skateboard and a cheese sandwich, I spy my driver. Saved! He pointed to two other gals and he said he thought one of them was me because they had red hair. I gave them half a glance and quickly retorted, "Dyed." Stupid red-head posers. My driver was soo hella funny that it made up for most of the stuff I went through.

I tell you, there are few things better at fixing sad panda face than the cool leather confines of a back seat, a bottle of spring water and a driver who loves Kevin Smith movies. We are off, speeding towards Stately Wayne Manor at last.

I guess I owe you an explanation for the Batman references. It will make things easier to follow if I allow you a peek inside my brain and how it works. First, I love Batman. I mean who doesn't unless you are a Godless Commie. Second, Roxy and Rex live in the vicinity of one of the houses that was used as the exterior for Stately Wayne Manor. I'm not telling you if it was the TV series or one of the movies. It's none of your business, but that's where the nickname came from. Also, it's cool. It's as simple as that.

Anyway, once I got to Stately Wayne Manor, SWM for short, Roxy and I went out for a drive in the new Batmobile. Okay, it was her new Mini Cooper Clubman S but it is the coolest car ever. I mean it has all these gadgets. Roxy gave up the lease on her previous SUV to buy this car. This car rocks. It's so much cooler than a Jag or any other poser car. It's chocolate and cream with leather seats, sunroof, satellite radio, interior night mood lighting that changes color with the flick of a button, keyless ignition, joy stick to control most features, blue tooth, heated seats, mpg calculator, (around 30 city/35 highway) and so much more. To paraphrase the Joker, "Where does she get those wonderful toys?"

Roxy reminds me that the back seats come out and the back double door access has a deeper storage area that can accommodate at least six bins. I was going to get a Saturn Vue as my next car but now... Hmm.

We decide to take the Batmobile out for a cruise around Pasadena when we stop to gas up. Picture this: two hippie chicks in multi-colored clothes that would fit right in at Woodstock. In fact, I'm pretty sure one of these women was at Woodstock. The other was probably conceived there. Suffice it to say, neither of these gals were anywhere near twenty. Why mention their age?

Because they were wearing micro mini skirts and NO underwear! Yes, you heard me right. The oldest of the pair bent over to pump her gas while the other bent over to pick up something she dropped, and they flashed the Netherlands to everyone at the Exxon, including the nice police officer.

There is nothing that will make you blind quicker than a shot of wrinkled vertical smiley in the morning. Officer "How Much Are They Paying Me," bless his heart, proceeded to write the ladies up for violating public decency AKA indecent exposure. I thought we were all going to start applauding. Our tax dollars at work, for once. Thank the Gods! No one needs to see what we did. By the way, these gals had never been to Brazil. On safari in deepest Africa, an entire hunting party got lost in those bushes and were never heard from again. I know, it's a painful mental picture, but at least now that I've shared with all of you, my pain is less, or at least that's what I keep telling myself.

Once we returned to SWM, it was time to play and forget about the horrid scene that had blasted its way into our brains. Anyone who said only kids play with toys has never partied with me or my friends. Xbox, PS2, PS3, Wii, and a variety of games for all these platforms awaited our gaming pleasure, along with Rex's excellent martoonis. I am a firm believer in mixing drinking with gaming. I think it improves my reflexes, or at least makes me care less when I lose or die. After a dinner of sushi, sake and cocktails we played Rock Band on the PS3.

I love being here!

THE DOUCHEMOBILE

This trip has been filled with many surprises. Aside from the flashing hippie women, I found out that Rex, that paragon of geek cool, has descended into the depths of douchedom. How do I know this? He told me. The conversation went something like this:

Rex, "I'm a douche."
Me, "What?"
Rex, "I'm a douche."
Me, "Why?"
Rex, "I bought a Porsche. It's a douche car."
Me, "Kinda...but it's cool. You are not a douche. In order to be a douche you need to be arrogant. You aren't arrogant. You're a nerd that got caught up in semi-douchedom."
Rex, "OK." (leaves for an hour – returns) "OK, now I'm a douche."
Me, "What?"
Rex, "I needed a car cover for when we are gone. The only one the dealership had has a huge Porsche logo on the hood so even if it's covered up you still know the car is a Porsche. It's so douchey."
Me, "You aren't a douche, but you could have just gone to Pep Boys."
Rex, "I tried. The cover they had didn't fit. The only car cover that fits is the one from the dealership. Hey, since Roxy is leaving you the keys to the Clubman, when you back it out, you'll remember my car is parked against the fence."
Me, "Don't worry, I won't hit your car. Don't be a douche."

Yes, it's now parked next to the Batmobile. I can't fault him too much. He broke down and did what most men only dream of doing and got a lease on a candy apple red Porsche. At least Rex has the good sense to be conflicted, a bit. Ladies: It's like having a fabulous diamond necklace and then wondering if you are wearing blood diamonds. Ah yes, did the acquisition of this piece of upscale bling cause the death and mutilation of hundreds of people? See? When you look at it from the female point of view, owning a race car with the aura of a micro-penis midlife crisis isn't so bad. I immediately nicknamed it "The Douchemobile."

It is certainly not Rex's fault that cool cars like the Porsche, the Lamborghini and the Ferrari have the reputation of being the "go-to" cars for aging men with tiny jimmies and something to prove. I've never known a guy who was able to afford a car like this before, so testing out this theory was a bit difficult. I do know one guy who has a cool Prowler, but his wife assures me his manhood is large, massive, dinosauric even, so I am eliminating the Prowler from this category. I am also discounting the Tesla because even though it's amazingly cool, most guys with tiny junk are too intimidated to drive an electric car.

So, is it just the ownership of said car that makes Rex think he's a douche? No, not really. I went out with Roxy to get an Aztec Mocha from Jones Coffee and when we returned we saw Rex had put a sun reflector thingy in the window of the Douchemobile. It has "Porsche" emblazoned on it along with the logo. I went inside and found Rex sitting by the TV.

"Why?" I asked. He hung his head in shame and said, "Yeah, I know. It's douchey. It's the only one that fits. They do it on purpose." Roxy chimes in with, "Did you see the frameable douchey certificate he got with the car?" Rex sputters, "No, and she never will and no one else will either because it's douchey!"

It seems when you buy a Porsche you get a certificate to prove you have entered the special, exclusive club of "powerful men." The certificate sports the Porsche logo, nice type, and lists the price you paid for said article of symbolic power. Of course, it is suitable for framing. Anyone who actually frames this certificate of shame and displays it (and you know there are people that do) is a Class A asshole of the highest degree. Rex was considering framing it and hanging it over the toilet as a joke but thought better of the idea.

Rex isn't a douche. The best way to tell is the fact that he realizes what a cool, douche car he has and isn't afraid to embrace it. Real douchey Porsche owners would get all pissed off if you even suggested they bought their car in a midlife crisis fog, wanting to impress a nineteen-year-old coed with more plastic in her body than Barbie, all in order to distract her from his miniscule wiener.

As luck would have it, the next day we were on our way to the airport when I saw a guy in a black Porsche. The license plate read "Black Shark." The guy wasn't too unfortunate looking, but the look in his eyes was unmistakable. Arrogance. Total and complete arrogance. This guy was a douche, though I have to admit I found myself drawn towards his doucheness and his car like a moth to a flamethrower. I had to pull myself away and give myself a reality check. Guys like this (a) only date models that look like ten year old boys, (b) always look at themselves in a mirror more than they look at you and (c) are douches.

At least now I have a solid example to give Rex of exactly how he's NOT a douche just because he wanted a cool car.

THE SILENCE OF THE SQUIRRELS

I returned from dropping off Roxy and Rex at LAX without a clue of what to do with myself for the rest of the day. Finally, I decided I could plan my social calendar for the rest of the week, play Xbox and drink. Drinking is a very urbane activity here at Stately Wayne Manor. It reminds me of Jay Gatsby standing on his lawn in Long Island, staring at the green light on Daisy's dock, only there is no water around here and Pasadena hardly qualifies as West Egg, but it sounds good.

So today's social calendar entry is:

"Drop off our Wyoming bound heroes at LAX, wait for the plumber, go to Jones for an Aztec Mocha, search for the secret bat pole that I'm sure connects to a super cool underground Batcave, have supper with Kitten and dress the dogs up in ridiculous costumes for my fun and amusement."

I'm sorry, didn't I mention the dogs? I am so remiss in my duties. Roxy and Rex have two wonderful dogs. Mongoose is a short-haired, medium-sized, black dog; a loveable mutt who looks a lot like her predecessor, Junior. Mongoose, or Goose for short, is a total attention whore. If anyone is getting any attention, she better be getting her share as well.

The other pooch in this picture is Alvin. Alvin's a black, male Cocker Spaniel and he worries. A lot. He worries if he's going to get fed, he worries if his toy will be still be there in the morning, he worries about the prime interest rate, he worries about conflict

195

in the Middle East. He just worries. It seems sad that such a small dog carries the weight of the world on his furry little shoulders.

What I worry about is how to get into the clandestine Batcave. I know it exists. I've seen it from a distance; there is Scotch in the Batcave, lots and lots of Scotch. Actually, you get to the Scotch cellar/booze cave via a door under the stairs to the second floor, but it's a lot more interesting to imagine a secret pole concealed behind a sliding panel. Now, if I can just get the Scotch cellar open, the booze is mine! I can party like Tara Reid on a low key Wednesday night bender.

I am determined to figure out a way to get in. The door is locked. Of course. My friends aren't crazy enough to leave me alone with their 40 year old Scotch. I hunt around, looking for keys under the furniture, behind books, and under rocks. I look for secret switches, moveable door parts, and then all of a sudden I spot something very suspicious.

I see a statue of Bugs Bunny. He seems out of place, really out of place. There are no other statues or ornaments around, and moreover, what grown person has a statue of Bugs just hanging around their foyer? Besides, the carrot in his hand appears to be pointing. What is it pointing at? I am running out of time. The sun is setting, I have to get ready for dinner. My girlfriend Kitten is coming over to pick up some hats I need her to repair and we are going to have a bite to eat. I have no choice but to abandon my search for now. As I climb the stairs, Bugs' receding figure mocks me in the gloaming. Bastard.

The sunset from the picture window is beautiful, but that serene image doesn't last for long. I spy them in the tree outside. The Squirrels. There are a lot of them, a ton, a platoon... Okay there are five, but still they look like a legion. They are sitting on the branches, looking into the house. They are just staring at me, yet again. Damn squirrels. I just hope they aren't planning some kind of rodent invasion. Just as I reach for my phone to call Homeland Security, they scramble up the tree, running off to God knows where. Perhaps they need to file a surveillance report with their superiors or maybe it's cocktail time at squirrel central.

Hours later, after having a fabulous Chinese dinner, accompanied by some devine pomegranate Martinis, I fall into bed with some leftover Chow Mein. Sad little Alvin was laying on the bed looking at me with those liquid brown eyes. He was just emoting, "I am really worried about you. There could be MSG in those noodles. I really should eat those for you."

Stop it! Stop it with the liquid brown dog eyes and the concern and the worry and the, "You know I am right. Your life is just a big Greek Tragedy, give me your food" look. I give up. The dog wins. I put away the Chinese food and give him a chewy.

Now he's worrying less, and I can sleep a little easier tonight.

MAGNOLIA AND ALVIN'S MALADY

So, the day dawns bright and full of promise. However I manage to spend most of it on YouTube finding 70's pop bands to torture my friend Jimmy with. It's not my fault that I have never been able to get on YouTube before this, and now I'm hooked. You see, at home, I still have a dial up connection, so YouTube takes too long to load. This video marathon started out like some kind of strange drug addiction, but now, after two days of dancing hamster videos, it's starting to get old. Well, except for the deranged poodle trying to have relations with a cat. It really amazes me how long it takes before the cat has enough of this dog humping its back. Damn, I've known cats that will slice your leg to ribbons if you pet them the wrong way. If that isn't bad enough, there is a video of a poodle and a stuffed rabbit; like I said, these are hours of my life I am never getting back.

So, after video surfing, I decide to take a refreshing walk around the neighborhood. I mean, it's a nice neighborhood, certainly not a place where you will be jumped by thugs for your cash and prizes. As I am walking back up "Mansion Row" I notice something odd. It's trash day and everyone has sent their trash bins down to the street for pick up. The rich have a lot of shit. I mean, how much trash do these people generate besides Paris Hilton and Tara Reid?

I do a quick mental calculation and figure at most, these huge houses contain two adults, two or three kids and a nanny. At the very least, there are only one or two adults living there. The majority of these homes aren't inhabited by the Brady Bunch and each house has a dumpster for their trash. A dumpster. These are the large black ones, just like the kind you find in back of a restaurant. Really?

Can you really fill a dumpster in a week if you aren't running a high-end eatery out of your guest house? Do they just sit around and figure out what to waste? Do they buy food just to bin it, so they have something for pick up each Friday? Do they fill the dumpsters with cases of empty booze bottles from their valet parking parties? But, wait, shouldn't those bottles go in the recycle bins since these people are also all socially conscious and shit? I'm at a loss and trying to understand the garbage habits of the wealthy has made me hungry.

I walk back to SWM, hop in the Batmobile and go to a local Italian deli for a sandwich. At this point, all I want to do is have a little bit of lunch, possibly roast beef on sourdough bread and relax with the dogs before I go out for more friend and booze laden fun later tonight.

Once I get back to the house, I have to make sure my food is close at hand and guarded since the dogs, ever vigilant, might mistake it for an intruder and eat it. Alvin heaves a sigh and looks at me meaningfully. I think he wants a bite of my sandwich. Fortunately, Goose is nowhere in the vicinity, or I would have a canine revolt on my hands. Alvin snakes his tongue out when I was distracted and kinda licks my sandwich. It reminds me of a little kid claiming a treat as their property by marking it with saliva. The licking trick is a classic.

I still eat it. I know, he licks his balls, but his mouth is still cleaner than most guys. I think guys should take that as a lesson. If a girl will swap spit with a dog and not you, there is a problem, and it's not with the dog.

After that refresher, I turn on the Wii Fit for my thirty minutes of yoga and aerobics. The stupid machine still says I am fat. According to its stupid BMI table I am one pound overweight. My Mii is now chubby. I hate myself. I have to fight an urge to get in the Batmobile and go back to Jones Coffee for another Aztec

Mocha and a blueberry cheese danish besides. I promise myself I'll work out tonight after my evening cocktail hour. Not that I'm that good at keeping these promises to myself, but I try and that's what counts.

Screw Wii Fit. I am on my way out of the house to meet my girlfriends at a trendy new club called Magnolia. Roxy told me about it, and since it is close, I decided it was worth a look. The website really makes this place look amazing. It's dark, baroque, trendy and brooding. It has all the promise of a hip place to hang out, but shouldn't I know better than to judge a book by its cover? I mean, how many romance novels has Fabio helped sell to straight women?

Initially, my gal pals, Amanda and Kitten, were both coming with me to share in trendy drink heaven, but Amanda's babysitter punked out at the last minute. How totally rude! What is with these people? Can we put her in the stockade and feed her bread and water for a week as punishment? Roxy told me to get to the club when it opens at 4:30pm but not to stay late or go on Friday or Saturday. So. with warnings in hand, Kitten and I get there around 5:00pm.

It's a small place with an outdoor bar area and two indoor seating areas. Seating is an eclectic mix of tables and couches, but the couches are all reserved. Of course, half of those reserved sofas were never used in the two hours we were there. Just for the record, I hate these poser clubs that post reserved signs on their good tables just in case Tara or Brittney decides to come to Pasadena for some cooch flashing. Great. We sit at a table with a good view of the bathrooms. Happy hour goes until 7:00pm, and includes some drink and food specials, so we throw ourselves into the fray with total abandon.

We start with the fruit and cheese plate. It is a lot of food for the two of us. Two large slices of triple cream brie whose rind did not taste like feet, a slice of parmigiano romano, goat cheese rolled in a ball and covered with nuts, six slices of baguette and two cheese toasted crackers. It was a pretty decent spread even though the fruit was only represented by a small bunch of sad looking grapes. We also ordered the coconut shrimp with a wonderful mango dipping sauce. The sauce isn't too sweet, and there is plenty to go around, so we don't run out half way through. I really hate it when that happens.

As far as drinks go, I could do without the cute sex names, but that's just me. I feel like an ass ordering an "X-Rated Pink Taco." Yeah, no lie. I start with the Magnolia. This signature drink is made with Citron Vodka, raspberries, lemonade and mint. Its tag line is, "Strong enough for a man but made for a woman." For a signature drink it is pretty pedestrian. They are lucky I ordered it in the first place since they are lifting the slogan from Secret deodorant. Does anyone really want to drink something that reminds them of deodorant? Apparently, I do.

Kitten orders some kind of chocolate martini thing. I don't recall the name, so it must not have been reminiscent of a toiletry product. For our second round we branch out into "funny name" territory. I go for the "Ruby Red Slippers" because it isn't a gross parody of the female anatomy and sounds kinda gay, which I like. I mean, who can resist a "friend of Dorothy" sounding drink. I should have. It was awful. Any one of my gays would have dumped this drink on the next tattooed, Emo boy waiter that passed our table. It tasted like cough syrup. Maybe it was Robitussin, I don't know but it was nasty. I drank it, just because at that point, I figured why not? Kitten ordered the kiddie book club sounding drink, "Buttery Nuttery Squirrel" or it could have been "Nuttery Buttery Squirrel." I lost my notes. It doesn't matter, because that one, while heavy sounding and being named for my nemesis, was actually pretty good.

To make things even better, we get hit on by an old guy. At first we thought he might be the owner of the club or a doctor or a film producer. No such luck. He is just an old guy with an average job. We discount his advances as not having enough potential for the amount of work involved. The little blue pill continues to be the bane of gold diggers everywhere. Why did science have to give eighty year old, half dead, guys boners? I just want to be nice to you and feed you soup. I don't want to have to play "Hop on Pop". No one should have to work that hard for your meal ticket.

I know, you are saying "Wait a minute! Didn't you just rant about hating gold digging women?" Yes. If they are young, bendy and wily like a rabid coyote. I found as you start to age, the sage words of Lorelei Lee, as embodied by the legendary Marilyn Monroe, come to mind. "Don't you know that a man being rich is like a girl being pretty? You wouldn't marry a girl just because she's pretty, but my goodness, doesn't it help?" However this is usually followed by the astute Monroe observation on older, monied gentlemen, "Why do they always look like unhappy rabbits?" I should have known he was a regular Joe by his less than rabbit-like appearance.

Sitting back by the loo, as we are, we watch one woman who waited too damn long to go the john and now finds it occupied. She stands there, doing the pee pee dance, desperately banging on the door. Failing to dislodge the potty parker, she finally gives up. I hope she doesn't go outside to whiz in the bushes. Since the toilets are only single occupancy, there's not even a men's room for her to crash. I fail to see how one unisex bathroom is enough for one club even if it is an intimate one.

We kill time and watch women with no fashion sense yammer at their boyfriends. If I could give them one piece of loving advice it would be, "Jesus, Mary and Joseph do not wear a bubble skirt with turquoise shoes and a lemon yellow feather boa, and for God's sake – shave your legs! I heard a rumor at the bar that the Destination Truth camera crew was on their way here to investigate a Bigfoot sighting. I would hate for them to make a scene trying to shoot you with a tranquilizer dart."

As if that wasn't bad enough, we find out why Roxy gave us the warning. After 7:00pm all the San Marino twenty-somethings invade. I think one gal even bought her clothes at Iilano Wear. She looks like a walking art project from Burning Man. We take that as our cue to go, leaving the bar to the bad mannered and morose ten year olds.

When I get home I discover that Alvin was sick all over the kitchen floor. I really don't need him buying his last biscuit before the 'rents get home, so I take him to the doggy doctor. It seems that the listlessness, the vomiting and the appetite fluctuations were a sign of ... depression. I now have to give the puppy uppers to help him deal with his mental condition. He misses his Daddy. Rex can't get home soon enough, because his dog is getting psychotic without him, poor little guy. Great. I am babysitting a chronically depressed dog that worries all the time. That explains his laying on the bed and staring at the wall. I should have noticed the symptoms. God knows, I've done that enough times myself.

I guess it's a good thing my cat is not alive to see this.

THE MONKEY SCREAMS AT MIDNIGHT

Well, yesterday my social calendar went something like this: pay the gardener, play BioShock on the Xbox 360, drive the Batmobile around Old Towne (turn donuts on the lawn of the Tournament of Roses Mansion while blaring "Hot for Teacher" on the sound system), drive to Disneyland and have dinner at Napa Rose.

I think I got to bed around 1:00am. Good news: the cops didn't catch me, and dinner was great. Bad news: Chef Andrew's Sous Chef tried to kill me. You see, I'm allergic to blue cheese. This was noted in the reservation. We ordered a large appetizer plate and there was a white substance on the fried oysters. It could have been many things, but the server tells me its blue cheese. Great. And it runs, so it has contaminated a few other pieces of this pricy dish. I am now torn between not wanting to waste food while actually wanting to eat the appetizer I ordered. Another one was made, but still I hate wasting food especially when I am someone's guest.

The lamb was wonderful as was the squash ravioli. However, the wine reduction sauce on the mushroom ragu was really too strong. I had to cut the lamb on the edge of the plate, out of the sauce. The sauce would overpower the lamb easily and the lamb was cooked so well, with so much flavor, that I didn't want to spoil it. Chef Scott, you are getting sloppy... Just because it's winter and you are featuring "hearty fare" does not mean you overpower your flavors. The ravioli was perfect but also light and the reduction completely buried the taste. Picking chanterelles out of the sauce and eating them with the pasta or the lamb worked perfectly.

Dessert was not in the cards for me because the pastry chef decided to make the desserts HUGE. They were actually two desserts in one. A cake with ice cream or a tart with a pot de crème. What if I just want pot de crème but not all the other stuff that I will never finish? Didn't you get the memo? The trend now is "fresh and smaller portions," or I should say "normal portions." The food was portioned normally, but the dessert needs to catch up. Have some choices that serve two, that is fine, but offer other desserts for those of us who want something sweet but not with a ton of calories. Thus ends my food review.

By the time I get home it's late. Really late. I fall asleep with no problem until I wake in the dark, jolted from my dreams by the screeching of a monkey. Yes, a monkey. I'm not making this up. It sounds a bit like this: "eeeeee eeee eeeeeeeeeee." In my half asleep stupor, I am confused as to where I am. Did I leave Disneyland last night and somehow woke up in the jungle, the zoo or Andy Dick's house? It was definitely a loud, shrill monkey scream coming out of the dark...from somewhere in the middle of the bed. Okay, this is a California King bed and the only other living critters in it with me are two dogs. They do not make monkey noises. I fumble for the light on the bedside table and flip it on.

It seems that Mongoose snuck her favorite toy into the bed with her. It's a monkey that has stretchy limbs and makes screaming howler monkey sounds when thrown, pulled or shaken. So, there was Goose, shaking the monkey. OK, that just sounded wrong, and she's a girl, but anyway, good God dog! Stop playing with your monkey. It's 4:00 in the morning! I grab the monkey, stuff it under the covers and go back to sleep. Now Goose is standing on me, all 40 pounds of her. She wants her monkey. Go away. I am not giving you your monkey. It was bad enough that you barked at Gordon when he came to pick me up. Go away. I push her off me, roll over and fall back to fitful sleep until...

The sun hits me in the eye. The clock says it's 6:00am. Goose is half standing on me, Alvin is looking at me with reproachful eyes. I feel bad, slightly bad, not totally bad since she did wake me up with the monkey. Maybe she needs to go outside. I get up, open the door in the bedroom that leads onto the balcony. It's freezing outside. She doesn't want to go out. Fine. I'm not going to heat up all of the outdoors for you. I decide since I am up now, I will just shower and get dressed.

I have to admit, waking up in sunny Pasadena, is so much better than waking up in dreary Squirrel Butt Arkansas. Have you ever been to Squirrel Butt? It's a sleepy town of 168 people with a post office, a McDonalds, a Dairy Queen and a Piggly Wiggly. It's a nice town, but the fertilizer plant does make things a bit ripe especially in the summer. Just take my word for it, Pasadena is way better.

Once a reasonable hour has arrived, I fire up the laptop and check my email. It seems Bank of America has sent me a missive regarding suspicious card activity. I figure it's because I'm in LA, but they have stopped my card, so I call to tell them, "Hey, it's me."

Umm, it wasn't me. Someone in Colorado took $500 out of my checking account at a Circle K (which was pretty much all I had in that account), then tried two more times to take out another $500, and then $600 at which point the bank froze the card. My problem? This is my only card. I don't have any other credit cards. I take a quick appraisal of my financial situation. I have $22 in cash, a Starbucks card with $20 on it and a Trader Joes gift card. When I return to the Oakland airport I have to pay to get my car out of the lot. I've got to eat and most importantly, I've got people to meet in the Garment District tomorrow at 9:00am. I am in deep trouble.

I ask the nice bank employee, working out of a call center somewhere on the planet, if I can get any of the money in my other account (which the thieves couldn't access). She says I have to call them back from the ATM, tell them how much money I am taking out, they will release the hold, I get the money and then they cancel the card and mail me another one. I won't lose any money, won't pay any fees but this is whole lot of trouble and I am pissed off.

I get in the car, drive to the bank and get money out of my savings account. At least now I have cash to tide me over, but this is still annoying me. I need some herbs, some candles and a whole lot of righteous anger. This person is so not going to like the massive case of intestinal parasites they are about to get. While I'm at it, a massive case of limp dick is also an appropriate punishment. Aw, has your "get up and go" gotten up and left? Oh, too bad - so sad - maybe you shouldn't be such an ass gasket and get your jollies robbing people, you piece of shit.

OK, I feel better now. I was going to go to Jones for an Aztec Mocha, but now it's Starbucks. In addition to the gift card, I found a free coupon. Stupid freakin' Starbucks. I have a love/hate relationship with them much the same as a junkie has with their crack pipe. There is a part of me that hates myself, but I just can't stop. I found better coffee at Jones, and I'm not even a coffee drinker. I crave the Aztec Mocha at Jones like Oprah craves deep fried pizza. Jones Coffee is my new Mecca. I wish I could go there, but this ass bite stole my money and I need to set a budget. Since I have a coupon, I can get anything at Starbucks for free. The lure of free is just too much to resist.

So, after all is said and done, I drive over to Starbucks on Fair Oaks. It's 10:30am and I'm doing the "leisurely LA stroll." This is the way women are forced to walk when it's hot out, we're in high heels, and our feet hurt. We are fabulous, and ladies don't show the pain.

I order a Venti Mint Mocha Chip Frappuccino and... they are out. OUT. It's 10:30am. What do you mean you're out? The gal tells me, "We've been making them all day, and we are out." All day? Umm, you open at what? 6:00am? Is that all day? How can you be out? I am so depressed. I post my mocha disappointment on Twitter and Facebook, and not even my friends sending me a list of all the Starbucks in the area can get me out of this funk now. I'm pouting.

I need to pull myself together. Perhaps a nice day at a museum will help, and it won't cost much money. In fact, I have a free pass for the Huntington. That would be nice. I better change my shoes though.

PIPPIN THE PARROT MADE ME HIS BITCH

I was going to go to the Huntington Library and Gardens today but decided to wait until tomorrow. The weather is beautiful and I want to enjoy it with some friends. I feed the dogs, grab the keys to the Batmobile and head off for an afternoon of fun with Dave and his family. You remember Dave from the night of the Irish Car Bombs? Well, I'm not planning on traveling down that road to perdition again. Besides, I'm driving Roxy's car and it wouldn't do to total it, taking out a bus load of nuns in the process.

I arrive at Dave and his wife Dawn's house in Orange County. Dawn is making chocolate chip cookies and what goes with cookies? Irish Car Bombs. I know, I know, don't judge me. Unfortunately we don't have all the fixings. So Dave and I hop in his Prowler and head to the store for Bailey's Irish Cream.

Now some of you might be asking, "What is a Prowler?" Well if Q designed a new car for James Bond, crossing a Formula One race car with a space age torpedo, the result would be the Prowler. It occurred to me that it's a shame Rex is out of town because we could get the Prowler and the Douchemobile together for a play date. I imagine it would be a fun car to drive. I know it's a fun car to be a passenger in. I doubt I will ever be able to own a car like this, and I know Dave wouldn't let me drive it on a bet. Did you know that this car was based on Plymouth's 1993 concept car? 1997 was the Prowler's debut model year and purple was the only color that was offered. No cars were produced in '98 but they started making them again from 1999 - 2002.

Oh My God. I'm turning into one of those douchey car owners without the benefit of actually owning a cool car. I so suck. I haven't even started drinking, and I am having flash backs to the douche in the black Porsche on the freeway mixed in with wandering the streets of San Jose. I push them out of my mind and concentrate on getting out of the grocery store in one piece. I mean, we just need booze and ice. Actually booze, ice and a can of spotted dick I saw in the foreign food aisle that I had to buy because, well, it's a can that says spotted dick. How could I not buy it?

By the time Dave and I return in the Super Agent Man car, a few more people have arrived. But before we can dive into booze, red meat and Dawn's cookies, Dave has something special he wants to show me. I figured it was a new laptop or a sword. Dave's really into low tech weaponry. He goes upstairs and comes back down with Pippin - a white-bellied caique, which translates into "Too Cute to Live" or perhaps "I Want to Eat your Face." Pippin is a wee green parrot with a white belly and a yellow/orange head. He really is wee, about 6" long, and seems pretty mellow. He is just a baby, only a year old, though for the rest of his life he'll be an eternally hyperactive three-year-old.

I was not raised around birds. I'm of the opinion that birds should be free to fly, cruising through the skies, shitting on my car and not stuck in a cage. I've also heard that the large parrots live over a hundred years, can be mean and have beaks so strong they can snap your finger with ease. Great. But Pippin isn't a large, loud, mouthy parrot screaming obscenities while smoking a cigar. Pippin is cute. He totally disarmed me. I never should have let my guard down. I know what happens when I do that with men and it's 31 flavors of bad.

Dave is walking around with the bird and asks me if I want to hold him. I figure, why not? What can happen? Pippin walks right up my arm, cocks his head and looks at me. He is so darling. I am enchanted. Now, I realize parrots are attracted by shiny bits, so I took my rings and earrings off before handling the bird. The last thing I needed was to have an earring ripped out of my ear or have him try to eat one.

He walks up to my shoulder, buries himself in my hair and starts preening. I start falling into that false sense of security I mentioned. Pippin starts bobbing up and down on my shoulder, nibbling at my hair. What is he doing? I seem to remember something from the Discovery Channel about when lizards bob up and down, it's part of a mating ritual. I remember this tidbit a tad too late to stop the inevitable.

Before I know it, this cute little bird grabs my throat and will not let go. This is not fun. Want to know what this feels like? Get a binder clip and clip it to your throat right above your Adam's apple. Go on, go find one. I know you've got one in a junk drawer somewhere. I'll wait...

Yeah, it's not pleasant. In fact, it fuckin' hurts! I panic. I count myself among the majority of mammals who takes any "going for the throat" movement as an attack. It is a measure of the esteem and love I bear my friends that I didn't snap Pippin's neck or toss him in the microwave. He wouldn't have been very tasty and was too small to make much of a snack anyway.

What did I do? I stand there yelling "GET HIM OFF! GET HIM OFF! GET HIM OFF!" It is very undignified and now that I think about it, the phrase was a bit ill-chosen for the situation. Dave detaches Pippin from my throat, and remarkably there is no blood or broken skin. I do have one hell of a hickey though. So why did the cute little bird nip me on the throat? I guess in Pippin's world, any critter who walks into his territory is another bird . I guess we are all really huge, weird looking birds, but cut him some slack, his brain is as big as an almond. I guess he thought I would make a good mate or that I was a threat. He was asserting his dominance. In parrot society one male has several females.

You heard me right, that little parrot just made me his bitch. I'm not sure what's worse? Having a squirrel try to run off with my underpants or having a little parrot hanging off my throat. I give up. I need a drink, and there is only one thing that will suffice. Yup, an Irish Car Bomb. Dave owes me that much. Pippin is sent back upstairs to his palatial cage and I am left to nurse my wounded pride with booze and warm cookies.

After an evening of red meat, Xbox and various conversations revolving around the tortoises in the back yard, I decide to call it a night. Here's a tip: don't ever try to take a basketball away from a huge tortoise. The one in Dave's backyard thinks it's his girlfriend. The gardener tossed the ball out of the way once when he was mowing the back yard and the tortoise charged him. Sure, it took him awhile, but he was pretty miffed. No one treats his fake girlfriend that way! Now that I think about it, there are some pretty unusual animals in this house.

Before I leave to head back to Stately Wayne Manor, Dave brings Pippin out to say good bye. He is very well behaved, rolls over on his back and cocks his head in an endearing way. Unlike his larger cousins, Pippin will only live about 30 years, but that is still way longer than a cat or a dog. He doesn't sing or talk, but he is a pretty boy. Okay, he gets to live.

I turned back and saw my bird boyfriend cocking his head and looking nonchalant.

SQUIRREL PEE – THE NEW WEAPON OF MASS DESTRUCTION

It was a lovely, if boiling hot, day at the Huntington Library here in beautiful Pasadena. I'm really missing out on culture in my life and thought this would help. Who am I kidding? I had a free pass from a friend, and I'm not going to let anything free go to waste. The Huntington isn't just a library. There are extensive manicured grounds, an art collection, and a tea house as well; it's a whole afternoon of civilized fun just waiting to be had. Due to the hellish heat, I spent the majority of my time in the main house that doubles as the art gallery. They have some wonderful new traveling collections including a Nicholas Hilliard miniature of Queen Elizabeth, which is part of an Elizabethan exhibit.

I while away hours looking at various master works, including some first folios of Shakespeare. After a few hours, I have had my fill of culture and venture outside to wander the vast grounds in search of shade and diversion. There are enough statuary-adorned nooks to keep me busy for hours. I avoid a run-in with the museum police by using my super stealth skills. Why is this necessary? I ignored the caution tape blocking a side road so I could go up to visit the graves of the Huntingtons. I figure you aren't really breaking the rules if no one sees you or cares.

I don't want to get thrown out of the Huntington Library, so after visiting the graves, I meander back to the main grounds to check out the new Chinese garden. They did an amazing job with it. This is just the kind of place where you would expect to bump into a handsome millionaire, fall instantly in love and live happily ever after. At least that's the way it always happens in the movies. I know those romantic films create unrealistic expectations, but I figure relationship scenarios are a lot like the lottery. You have to play to win. I try my best to look alluring while reading my civilized book in the shade of a blossoming tree. I'm a lovely flower and I don't want to burn my delicate skin.

Who am I kidding? I shouldn't be outside at all. I got a big ass sunburn yesterday, before Pippen tried to kill me, or mate with me, or whatever was happening in his sick little bird brain. So, unfortunately, today I am a loser in the millionaire fiance sweepstakes. After giving Alan Rickman, or any other eligible bachelor, a chance to sweep me off my feet, I decide to pack it up and head for home. It was a nice afternoon, but I have a Doctor Who marathon waiting for me back at Stately Wayne Manor. This is the new Doctor not the festive, multi-colored scarf wearing Doctor that scared me as a child.

On my way back to the house I swing by Jones Coffee for an Aztec Mocha Latte. I'm ready to settle in for some relaxing entertainment before Roxy and Rex return this evening. I have writing to do and Doctor Who watching. I've been working out with the Wii Fit every day, but the infernal machine still calls me fat. Just barely fat but still fat. I'm carrying on a love/hate relationship with the Wii Fit. It's almost enough to make me want to drive into Old Towne and buy a box of French pastries to eat with my latte. Eat hot death Wii Fit Monkey!

I restrain myself, drink my latte and start to relax when Alvin starts going nuts. He's running around, barking his fool head off. This means only one thing in my mind - squirrels. I think the heat has been keeping them in a hole somewhere, but here's one fat, cheeky bastard, swaying on a branch, taunting poor Alvin. I call to Alvin, hoping to get him to come back over to me, but Mongoose is trying to drink my latte, and I've got to deal with her first. In all this confusion, Alvin makes a bee line for the shaded arbor with the table and chairs underneath. The squirrel leaps onto the wooden arbor, angles its fat butt over the edge and pees on Alvin's head!

What is it with squirrels relieving themselves on pets in my care? I am still trying to process this. I didn't witness a long stream of hot, yellow pee come from the evil beast's nether region. I saw barking dog, mocking squirrel, hanging squirrel butt, barking dog, dog with wet spot on head, wet spot the size of a nickel on the stones, squirrel scampering away. The only possible conclusion? The deranged squirrel pissed on Alvin's head!

Rex is going to be so upset. I am incredulous. I sniff Alvin's head. I know, it sounds gross, but I do it anyway for the sake of science. I stop short of tasting the wet spot. I'm not that hard core of a CSI. His fur has a slight odor, but it could just be wet dog. It's not gamey and strong like cat pee. Maybe that reflects the squirrel's diet. God, listen to me dissecting the subtleties of squirrel pee.

I grab Alvin, lead him into the kitchen and wash the pee off his head. He just sits there, sad and dejected. I feel so bad for him. I know he was just trying to keep the world safe from the evil squirrel hordes. Now he has a new thing to worry about, and it's all my fault. I know the rodents sneaked in that scamper-by peeing just to get back at me.

I suck. The squirrels suck. Poor Alvin.

THE TWO COREYS AND ROCK BAND DON'T MIX

Roxy and Rex arrive back in town none the worse for wear from their foray into the hinterlands of Wyoming. I have a feeling they spent their time in the more sophisticated climes of ski chalets, espresso bars and drag clubs. The parts of Wyoming I have seen have included desolate roads, bad beer and locals with no concept of dental hygiene.

That evening we decide to order out for Chinese food, whip up a batch of martinis and fire up Rock Band. I still suck at drums. It's a good thing they have an extra guitar controller because I hate the virtual crowd booing and tossing virtual fruit at us. After an hour of martini enhanced playing, which I swear helps my reflexes, we are still going strong. The clock chimes midnight and with Roxy exhausted after the plane ride, she gives up and goes to bed. Rex and I, still fueled on Batcave martinis stay up to watch a reality show called The Two Coreys.

Oh my God! Train wreck doesn't even begin to describe the debacle we were subjected to. If you think Jerry Springer is bad, you haven't experienced the worst of the reality genre. I don't even know how to explain this show to you, but I'll give it a shot.

The Two Coreys, as the name states, stars Cory Haim and Corey Feldman. These aging former child stars are pseudo famous for the movie Lost Boys and some really bad D list teen movies of the 1980's. They were both sexually traumatized by an infamous person who appears to have a proclivity towards young boys, toys and primates. These kids didn't have a chance. As a result of early stardom and disturbing monkey attacks, they are doubly screwed up.

It appears that Feldman has moved past this childhood shock. He's married, has a pretty stable life and career. He really comes off as not wanting to be involved with this train wreck that used to be his friend. His wife, who also functions as his manager, seems to be pushing him to continue this idiot show for the dough.

Haim is the most pathetic, sad waste of a human being I've seen in some time. His moods vary bouncing around from happy to moody, bitter to crazy, and everything in between. He wants to make up for all the shit he put his friends through with his drug use and insanity but then can't understand why no one wants to hire him. He constantly questions his motives and thinks himself self-serving and over dramatic.

We watch two episodes, but at this point, I was laughing so hard and had so many martoonis that I really couldn't give you a coherent breakdown of the show. We declared that enough scary reality entertainment for one late night and went to bed.

*****

The next morning over coffee, Rex says to me, "Were we watching that Corey thing last night? That was a freak show - what I can remember of it." So, here is what I suggest the next time you feel like crap: watch that show and then thank the Gods you're not Corey Haim.

Later that afternoon, I fly back to Oakland. It was an uneventful flight. No strange fashion disasters, no covert squirrel attacks. I am feeling fortunate. The house is still in one piece, although my plants are near dead. I have emails to catch up on, so I try to log onto my dial up from my PC and... I can't! Why? Because my Netscape bill was direct billed to my ATM card. However, when I had to cancel that card on the 5th because of that criminal butt munch who hacked my account, I had forgotten that I had bills linked to that account. Now I have no Internet. Bugger.

Whole Foods has Wi-Fi but frowns on you camping out for eight hours straight to get email, apply for jobs and work on writing, so they only give you two hours of internet time. That screws me. What also screws me up is my stupid, freaking Bill Gates Microsoft Hotmail account. I have that address for job stuff exclusively. Guess what email account I cannot access? Yup - hotmail. It must be a cookie issue or an alien invasion or something equally nonsensical. Now I have no idea if anyone has sent me an email about a job. I fuckin' hate this program, and Bill Gates - you suck! I set up another job related email account on Yahoo this time and start correcting my resumes. The fun just can't wait to hit me in the face like a soggy noodle.

I'm praying my new ATM card will come today or tomorrow so I can give the new card number to Netscape, get my Internet back and be able to have more flexibility with Wi-Fi access. This 8am - 10am at Whole Foods is constricting, but I shouldn't complain. At least this leaves more time for idiot shows like <u>The Two Coreys</u>.

So good to be home...

WII FIT CRUSHES MY SOUL AND THE TRAP DOOR BEGGAR

Today I am trying to write, look for work, and examine my feelings about the Japanese, but I just end up getting all pissed off. Why am I pissed at the Japanese? The reasons are numerous, but it's mostly because they invented Nintendo and the Wii. I know, I know, Japanese gaming systems have brought so much joy to so many people. Wii was fun when I was playing Rayman Ravin' Rabbids at my sister's house. It's oddly satisfying to hit virtual bunnies, and smacking demented alien rabbits from outer space is right up my alley. But now, thanks to Roxy, I have Wii Fit. I figured nothing could be better than using a game system to exercise and get into shape. Oh, if I only knew.

The first thing I do after unpacking is finish hooking up the Wii. Everything is going fine. The cords are color coded. I mean, a blind parrot could do this, and then the strangest thing happens. The screen starts talking to me. Not out loud but it starts having an on-screen conversation with me. It asks me to give it a name just like a puppy or your boyfriend's Johnson! Yes, it wants a name. I am stumped.

If I name it Chauncy after my dead cat I would just sound crazy. If I name it after a Disney Princess, that would sound too weeny. So I go for my new hot crush of the year. No, not Jesus! I name my Wii "The Doctor" because David Tennant is hot. Okay, I did try "Capt. Jack" first because Captain Jack Harkness is dreamy, and he's an equal opportunity dog. Women, men, aliens, plants, doesn't much matter to Capt. Jack. But I was afraid (since I only had ten characters to play with) that people would think Capt. Jack was for Sparrow, and then I would have to shoot myself in the head. I like Jack Sparrow, but with all the Jack Sparrows running around these days it just makes me cry. So, The Doctor it is.

Next I set up my Mii. This is the little avatar that will represent me. I look like a little tramp, kinda, but at least I am not fat. Not until I get Wii Fit installed that is. I decide to put in Wii Sports and do a little bowling, because I am decent at that. I do alright for a novice virtual bowler. I only score one strike. No scratches. I know, it's not great but up until now I've only bowled on occasion. It's not something I actively seek out. My past has included driving to bowling alleys complete with bad beer, scary rental shoes and an atmosphere that smells of lost dreams. I thought virtual bowling would be better. It really wasn't with the exception of the shoes and the beer.

So, after that disappointing showing, I decide to move up in the realm of virtual athletics. I am hunting around on the menu when I find it. There is a button labeled "Wii Fitness." I click on it. I should really avoid clicking on anything having to do with exercise. It always ends badly.

While this abbreviated version of the fitness program has no way to weigh you, it tests your "balance and stamina." How does it do that? Well, you play three games and afterwards the Machine of Doom calculates your Wii age based on your performance. So first up is baseball. I sucked at this in school. I always got picked last, so I wasn't holding out hope of a very positive outcome.

You get ten opportunities to hit the ball. The first seven pitches I missed. On the eighth pitch I got a hit and on the ninth pitch I hit a home run. The tenth pitch I missed. Well, I figure it was tons better than I ever did in school. Next up is bowling. I did pretty well considering I was just playing this game and I haven't even been drinking. The last game up was tennis. I did fairly well. I hit most of the serves. In fact I only missed two out of ten. After all of this trauma, the computer calculated my Wii age. What did I get? Twenty-three? Thirty-five? I wish. No, according to the Machine of Doom I'm seventy-eight. Yeah, SEVENTY-EIGHT. After flashing this result in letters that appear to be a foot high, that machine has the nerve to say "Hey! Great Job!"

SEVENTY-EIGHT? FUCK YOU Wii. Gee, I haven't even gotten on a scale and already it's making me feel bad about myself. Maybe this is a plan by the Japanese to take over America by lowering our self-esteem and addicting us to their video products. Hey, it's a theory, but I like it. I'm watching you Japan!

I really thought the machine had calculated this all wrong. I mean, I played Wii Fit when I was at Stately Wayne Manor and things weren't that bleak. Who am I kidding? I exercised like a madwoman and what happened? Do I get Buns of Steel in 30 days? Can I grate cheese on my rock hard abs? Nope. The computer calls me fat and makes my lazy ass Mii character chubby. Okay, I am barely fat. In fact, one day I dipped down to Normal. The fat end of normal, but at least the Wii wasn't bitching at me when I dipped into the "normal" zone. Yeah, that whole BMI index is flawed anyway. It never was intended to be used like this and it just adds to our national weight obsession.

As my weight tends to go up and down thanks to birth control pills and mayonnaise, I keep thinking that I can drop ten pounds in a week with this Wii if I want to. LOLOLOLOL!! Whew! Yeah, like that's even possible. You see, this is why I'm pissed at the Japanese. They tempt me with promises of fun and easy weight loss, anime, fabulous food and twee fashion. They make me feel dependent on them for my entertainment and future happiness. I hate feeling dependent on anyone or anything.

When I got my Wii from Roxy and Rex, I called my sister and got game suggestions from my twelve year old nephew. My sister tried to convince him to send me the games he doesn't play anymore. He didn't know if he should because he "might" want to play them again. Sometime. I told him I would bring them back for Christmas or I would trade him my super cool grown up games that Mommy won't even let him see like Leisure Suit Larry. He asked what that game involved and sissy took the phone away.

Spoiled sport. I mean he's twelve and they are just animated boobies...

OK, I'm a terrible parent, which explains why I'm not one. I'd let my kids play games with animated boobies and not have a problem with it. I also am way too vain to ever be pregnant. I think looking like you swallowed a beach ball is really unattractive. Also pushing a Miata out of my vagina is not appealing in the slightest. Please save your hate mail for someone that cares. If you would like my uterus, since I'm not using it, I will gladly ship it to you if you pay for the surgery.

*****

So, today I got up at 6am to go out to the Laundromat in Piedmont before torturing myself with another round of Wii Fit madness. I put the clothes in the washer, dashed out to Starbucks for a latte and thought about going across the street to Posh Bagel. I mean what says Sunday morning more than a nice bagel and cream cheese? I couldn't do it. Why not? The trap door beggar. You see, there is an alley next to Posh Bagel, and lurking in this alley is a guy with a cane, wearing a trench coat, hidden, out of direct view, BUT when someone pulls up to the bagel shop or walks past it, he pops out of the alley like a trap door spider to beg for money. It gives me the creeps.

I watch him from the safety of the Laundromat, trying to determine if there is a pattern to his covert assaults on bagel customers and J-random pedestrians. Was it safe? Was the coast clear? Could I go to Posh Bagel? The sidewalk looked clear - oops, there he popped. Bugger.

Men, let me give you some advice, it's just not seemly to be talking to a lady, especially an unaccompanied lady, when you have not been introduced. It's creepy. It's especially creepy to spring out at people. I particularly hate being bothered/talked to/hit up for money by trap door beggars who pop out of alleys and discourage you from going to a bagel shop on a Sunday morning with the change you scrounged from the sofa cushions. I mean, I deserve a bagel paid for with my hard earned sofa change!

My mother would say, "You don't really need that bagel." Well, I also don't need an HDTV but that doesn't mean I don't want it, but in this case, I guess she's right. Carbs have always been my enemy. I drop much more weight when I keep away from bread and pasta. It really sucks. Perhaps one day they will invent a bagel with half the carbs that still tastes good. Oh, and one day I will get to meet Alan Rickman and he will want to marry me.

Hey! We are all entitled to our dreams.

MY DAY IN COURT

Well today is the day I head to bankruptcy court. This is so strange. On the one hand, I know it will be a relief to get this all behind me, and on the other hand there is this lingering feeling of shame. It feels like a dirty little secret you've tried to forget since childhood, like Uncle Squingy wanting you to go fishing for Tootsie Rolls in his pants pocket.

When you declare bankruptcy, all of your debt is discharged. You can't pick and choose what to keep and what to give up. All your credit cards go. This was a good thing and a bad thing for me. I had a Disney Visa with Chase that I wanted to keep, but I was behind on the payments. I called Chase and wanted to work with them. They responded like loan sharks with a prison gang mentality. I was told I could pay $200 now and $300 in two weeks or they would take me to court. I tried to explain to the jail house thugs that if I had that kind of money, I wouldn't be behind. What did they expect me to do? Sell crack to school kids? The "customer care" monkey didn't care. I informed him in my most reasonable voice that they could get $30 a month until I got back on my feet, or I would declare bankruptcy and they would eat the whole thing. He was unmoved.

I am now getting a tiny bit of perverse pleasure out of screwing Chase since they were so inflexible and rude to me. I am ashamed and appalled to be forced to default on my Mastercard, which has been in good standing for the past twenty years. They don't deserve to get screwed, but the rule is all the cards must go. It's like a perverse fire sale.

My car was paid off anyway, but it was my understanding you are usually able to keep the car, unless it's expensive and over the top like a Rolls or something. I guess the court figures, if you have any hope of getting a job, you are going to need a car. At least in California.

I was also paranoid that the court would make me sell all my worldly possessions like my Barbies or my Grandmother's ring. Well good news, unless those Barbies are cast in solid gold, you're good. The court is really only interested in things like second homes, boats, a fleet of antique cars, huge plasma screen televisions, you know, things they could actually sell for real money. They couldn't care less about your books, clothes, toys or porn collection. I know that's a big relief to many of you.

I walked the half hour to the court house, went through the metal detector and headed up to my court room. I was ushered into to a dingy room that smelled like despair where a dozen other sad and desperate people milled around trying to look nonchalant. As I waited for my attorney to show up, I checked out the roster on the door which listed the people the judge would see in this hour. Yeah, this hour. I found out from my attorney that in the past, an Alameda County Bankruptcy Judge would usually see six or eight cases a day. Now the judge sees about forty a day. Explain to me again how this isn't a depression?

I was told we would be herded into a room and when my name was called I would go to the front of the room with my attorney and talk to the Judge at a table. Umm, a table? Yes, this is the kinder, gentler court. It's not a court room, it's a meeting room. The judge isn't all intimidating, sitting on a raised podium with a scary black robe, a wig and a hammer. She's a nice, older lady you could have a latte with at Starbucks. You sit at a table with her instead of behind a rail looking up at her. Maybe she would give me motherly advice about my finances and men while we had milk and cookies? See? Don't you feel better about being in penury already?

You still have to swear to tell the truth, the whole truth, and nothing but the truth. The judge asks you questions about your assets, your debts, if you want to keep your house and other relevant things. In my case, my house was being surrendered to the bank. Your creditors are all notified of your impending court date so they can show up. I have no idea why they would want to do this, since the Court frowns on creditors mocking and tossing rotten fruit at the petitioners. The judge is very cordial, grants my bankruptcy and wishes me luck. I'm just glad for the whole thing to be over with and for the fact we no longer have debtor's prison.

My attorney informs me that the court has now wiped out all of my debt, including what I owed on the house. It has now been surrendered to the mortgage company. She told me it could take the bank another six months to a year to sell it, so I had some time to find a job and get back on my feet again. She told me her sister-in-law was in her house for two years after her divorce. I just felt a large weight leave my shoulders. Am I free of all the burdens I have been carrying? Not hardly. I still need a full time job so I don't have to subsist on government cheese. I mean, President Bush keeps saying the economy will improve much faster if we only give the rich companies more bail-out money.

I fail to see how this helps me, but hey, what do I know?

THE DAYS OF RUM AND ROSES OR NEW WAYS TO CELEBRATE BIRTHDAYS

Okay, so as of 8:53am, I am officially a year older. Whee! Happy Birthday to me. As it got closer to my natal day I thought about many things. Some of my friends celebrate their birthdays with joy and childlike exuberance, some with fear and loathing, others with grasping avarice. I've never seen the sense in the declaration of, "I am celebrating my birthday all month, so here is my not-so-subtle hint to everyone to buy me shit. Here is a list with websites and pictures of what I want." I find that classless, tasteless and annoying.

A very wise woman named Linda Underhill once told me; presents aren't asked for or demanded, they just appear. If you get presents every day, they wouldn't be special. Okay, she was talking about sex, but the same principle applies.

I decide, instead of being a birthday month hog, I will only have a twelve-day celebration because twelve days is far less ostentatious than a whole month of birthday mayhem. I think maybe I will write a song, a little jingle, after it's all over about what silly thing I did for each day. Yes, like the annoying Christmas song. It could be entertaining. Fun birthday activities don't have to cost money. I could go to the lake and flick garbanzo beans at the kids that torment the geese. That's always fun. 10 points if you can bounce a bean off their wee heads! I think I could occupy myself for twelve days with various treats and bouts of mayhem.

I figure since my birthday is on a Tuesday, it's already a little pedestrian. The poem I learned as a child does say that Tuesday's child is full of grace. I try to be graceful, but I mostly trip over my feet. Actually, I was born on a Sunday. According to the rhyme "And the child that is born on the Sabbath day is bonny and blithe, and good and gay." Yup, that's me – good and gay. Now I just have to plan some fun, stupid things to keep me in book fodder more than anything else.

Explain to me again why we do this? I mean when we were little it was different. You would have a party with streamers and balloons and cone shaped hats. You would have cake and ice cream and a pile of presents and someone would cry for some dumb ass reason. You might get to go somewhere fun and exciting, like a pizza parlor. Let's see, what were the highlights of birthday parties I had as a kid?

• Pizza party at Straw Hat. I love mushroom pizza.
• Playing "Pet the Kitty." Get your minds out of the gutter, we were eight!
• A green glitter Schwinn bike with a silver banana seat.
• Cutting my cake before my sister. You see, my sister's birthday is the day after mine. One year my parents got us a sheet cake. Half said Happy Birthday Deirdre and the other half said Happy Birthday Nadine. I got to cut into my half first so she got a used cake. I guess that kinda sucks, but when you're little you so don't care. Unless, of course, you are the kid with the other half of the cake.
• Barbie things.
• Bringing cupcakes to school.
• Wearing a crown made of corrugated sea foam green paper decorated with a "5" in silver glitter and not taking it off for a week. Hey! I was in Kindergarten.

As I got older, parties got stranger, like the Jaws party. We were young teens back then. We all went to see Jaws. I screamed and threw my popcorn in the air when the opening music came on. I had an ice cream cake decorated with a shark eating a swimmer. There was red icing under the top layer of frosting and there were

M&Ms in the cake, so when you cut into it, it bled and things popped out. It was awesome.

Then, as time passes, the parties tend to peter out. I can't remember any kind of birthday party during college. Perhaps there was one involving Brown Cows in dirty glasses from Merle's Drive In or Rick Dunn and the dildo ray gun, but I am not sure. That whole period of my life is another book entirely.

I've had to face the fact that when you grow up your birthday just becomes another day. You may do something fun or special, but you sure as hell aren't running around wearing a cardboard crown with "35" written on it in glitter. I've had birthdays when I was totally broke. Not quite Tiny Tim broke but close enough. Once when I was living in Pasadena I went and got a scoop of Robin Rose ice cream as a treat. It was raspberry truffle. That was my entire birthday present to myself and let me tell you, it was amazing.

As time rolls on, women around you can get annoying. You know the ones. As my friend Susan likes to say, "The ones who count their money in public." These are the chicks that just like to brag for the sake of scoring points in some dumb ass game no one else is playing. It usually involves something along the lines of, "My boyfriend/husband got me a sports car, a diamond tennis bracelet, and a trip to France, for my birthday. What did you get? Oh yeah, you don't have a man. I'm so sorry."

Shut it bitch! Okay, so I've never had a guy buy me presents like that. So I chose poorly in the past and have decided to marry Jesus in the future and he isn't into material items. MY fiancé can make wine appear out of thin air, as much as I want, so there! Do I win?

I guess, now that I think of it, the only gifts I got from boyfriends were things that I ultimately paid for so that really doesn't count. The fact that I'm done with those pieces of trash is actually a really good present. Knowledge and experience are far more valuable than baubles any day.

So, today for my lunch hour I walk over to Fenton's, get an egg salad sandwich to go and a petite cup of toasted almond ice cream to eat while I am waiting. It is luscious and creamy and makes my mouth happy. Now how's that for an experience?

I do consider inviting friends for a dinner at my new favorite dining establishment, but I decide against it. I hate those parties. Why? I know what it is like to receive those dreaded e-mail invitations to a friend's fondue extravaganza or some similar birthday shindig. It always turns into a "come eat in an expensive restaurant and pay for yourself and part of the birthday person's food and their Chivas and whatever else they are drinking" party. I am usually poor and can't afford it, so I don't go. I want to be able to have a birthday dinner with my friends, but I would pay for everyone so I could enjoy their company and they wouldn't feel uncomfortable because they couldn't afford to go. Right now, though? Not happening. Perhaps one of these days I will be able to do that.

My friend Roxy and I did that once on a smaller scale. We had a joint birthday party at Lucky Baldwin's Pub in Pasadena, at their old location. We paid the bartender a pile of money, gave our guests stickers and told the staff that anyone with the kitty pumpkin sticker could drink on our tab. Once the tab was up, they paid for their own drinks. We included the tip, but we knew that people would also tip again so the bartender made out well. The bar threw in plates of cold cuts and cheese and bread and we brought cake. The booze lasted from noon to around 5pm and then some people stayed for pub food and the pub quiz. It was brilliant!

So, maybe I will try to finish my computer game or have that ice wine I was saving. I think I will pick up something at Whole Foods, or I can drink the massive amounts of beer and wine that are mocking me. I'm sure I can think of something low cost and fun to do for my birthday.

After all, I am pretty inventive.

I WAS KIDNAPPED BY GAYS

Well, Saturday was shaping up to be an overcast, "Let's sit around being a lump" kind of day. That was until The Kevins showed up. It seems they were in The City for a week and decided I needed rescuing. I just could not stay home and stare at a steel gray sky. They announced we were going to the Spa and that was all there was to it.

Who are The Kevins? The Kevins are from Newport Beach; however, they migrate to the Bay Area for regular trips to the Wine Country. They are tanned, stylishly dressed and have a Bichon Frise named Winston. Winston is routinely emasculated with the application of various bows and powders. I tried sticking up for the dog once but was assured that daddy's little man loved the widdle bows. Okay, they didn't say "widdle" but it was implied, and the bows were wee. They were not butch bows.

Winston is new to me. For years they had a Boston Terrier named Reggie who was just too cool. He would sport spiked collars and Coach leather dog accessories. I miss Reggie. Winston takes some getting used to. He looks like a walking Q-tip.

However, I'm not here to pick on poor disadvantaged Winston. For this foray into spa land, Winston stayed at home with his nanny. Yes, the dog has a nanny, don't judge. The Kevins swung by my house in their shiny new Lexus and off we went to Changes Spa in Walnut Creek for a few hours of massages and facials.

I must say that after the whole "going to court" experience and not being tossed into debtor's prison, this was a nice change of pace. On our way to the spa we discussed the newest eateries, their recent trip to Florence and what a train wreck Lindsey Lohan is. There is nothing that brings your spirits up faster than focusing on the misfortune of the rich and stupid.

Spas are wonderful. I don't know if we should give the Romans credit for them, but this is one of the best ideas in human history. We were shown to our respective locker rooms, changed into our fluffy robes and met back up in a tastefully decorated room where we soaked our feet in elevated stone basins of warm water and perfumed salts. We sipped white wine while Kevin A. regaled us with the wonders that are Florence. A trip to Italy also sounds like a very good idea right now.

After our foot soaks, we were whisked off to separate rooms for our pampering. I must say that after the Oxygen facial and a full body massage, my back is now back in alignment, my tweaked hip is better and my skin is soo smooth. I guess this is what being real estate agents turned entrepreneurs means; a life of luxury cars, massages and fluffy dogs. I'm not complaining. I can think of worse ways to spend an afternoon than lying on a table, drunk, wrapped in seaweed. Wow, that kinda sounds like the Little Mermaid after a rough night at the clam bake.

Afterwards we went to lunch at Le Cheval for excellent Vietnamese food and relaxing conversation. I adore the Kevins. They have been together so long they are starting to look like each other. I've always felt more comfortable around gay men. Face it, they are just more fun. They shop with you, go to spas with you, tell you if you look a fright and tell you when you look fabulous. They have lovely homes, great style and witty banter. You can go out, raise hell and not have to worry about them wanting to get into your knickers later because "they bought you a cheese pizza." Gay men aren't that crass and they aren't interested in what's in my knickers. Gay men are liberating to the straight, single gal. They're our security blankets. They make you feel that the world is all beautiful and lovely and filled with joy which, it really is.

Years ago, my sister was concerned about all the gay guys I hung out with when I was younger. She thought if I only went out with gay men I would never find a husband. Well, no husband yet so maybe she has a point. Is it any wonder why I would run back to my gay friends? All the good, straight men are married or taken.

So, on the way back to the car, we decided to pop into Starbucks to get a latte. While we were standing in line, we saw this couple come in. She was about 5'8", 105 pounds, long blond hair, not hot, not pretty - kinda funny lookin'. It was a very "Fargo" moment. She wasn't ugly but she was just... funny lookin'. Gangly, like an insect with an annoying laugh and horse teeth. The guy was about 5'10", 200 pounds, orange fake tan, bleached hair with dark roots and teeny shorts with a muscle shirt.

The Kevins' opinion, "Gay, so gay, doesn't want to admit it but June is bustin' out all over gay. With a fugly beard and yeah, she was kinda funny lookin'." Why am I remarking on shallow things such as people's looks? Well, your outward appearance is the first thing people see and judge. Second are your actions. Now I could have gotten past the ill-chosen wardrobe or the funny lookin' thing with great conversation or quirky but cool interests. But, nope, these people had the social interest of paint drying. Here's an example of their strange, alien conversation:

Insect Girl, "Omygoddidyouseethaticouldn'tbelieveit." Yes, all in one whiny breath.

Orange in the Closet Gay Guy, "Huh, yeah."

O kay. I'm sure these two get laid, and I want to know why. I haven't had sex since the last Mr. Wrong was tossed to the curb, and it's just not fair. I'll bet even Winston, the walking Q-tip gets some. At least I have my wonderful gay friends to show me there's more to life than bad sex; like cute shoes, yummy food and spa days. Their company is even better.

Straight men always end up disappointing me.

DEIRDRE SARGENT

ON THE FIRST DAY OF CHRISTMAS SOME GERMANS GAVE TO ME, A KITTEN IN A TALL TREE

So, it's been awhile since Chauncy passed. A respectable mourning period has gone by and I now have a new cat. Actually, she's a kitten. My German friends Andy and Beth were finding homes for a litter of insane Maine Coon kittens. They breed them cute but crazy over there. Beth kept telling me this particular kitten was "the sweet one." She had a "mellow personality." "She will just sit on your lap and she doesn't do anything crazy like the rest of them." Remember when P.T. Barnum said, "There's a sucker born every minute?" He was right. I have no idea why I trusted the Germans. The last time I left them to their own devices, Andy presented me with a replica of Notre Dame carved entirely out of cheese that he made on a bet.

I thought, "How bad can it be?" I've never had a kitten before, but they're so small. How much trouble can they really cause? I do know kittens have a chemical in their blood, similar to LSD, that makes them hyper, frantic and fuck-ass crazy. It seems to be a defense mechanism to make them harder to catch in the wild. But this kitten was so sweet and mellow and full of the cuteness. At four months old and consisting of only four pounds of fluff, this is not a hard thing to do.

So I took the kitten. She was wee and fluffy and fit in my hand. I named her Alia after Alia Atredies from the book <u>Dune</u> by Frank Herbert. <u>Dune</u> is my Bible. In the book, Alia was called

234

Abomination by the Bene Gesserit sisterhood, and she was known as St. Alia of the Knife to her crazy religious followers. The moniker "Abomination" seemed to fit this kitten. You see, one of the genetic quirks of many Maine Coons is they are polydactyl. No, they aren't dinosaurs. They have multiple toes. Alia has six on each of her front paws. Abomination doesn't even begin to cover it.

Yes, I know! I am begging for trouble by naming her Alia. Alia was crazy and possessed by the spirit of her grandfather Baron Harkonnen. Well, it seems the kitten has taken this to heart. There are times when The Baron has decided to manifest himself through her insane possessed behavior. Don't believe me? Well, there was the time when, for no apparent reason, she decided to pee in a bag containing a bottle of wine then look surprised.

"How did that happen? I certainly didn't pee in that bag!" was written all over her face. Then she ran off, leaving wee pee paw prints on the floor as evidence of her misdeed.

She has not yet learned that we don't get up at 4:30am to dance on Mommy's face. She's a bit of a face sitter, which Chauncy never was. She also burrows under the covers, which he also never did. I thought Alia would never be able to get up on my bed since it's so high. Yeah, I should have counted on the hyper crazy kitten figuring out how to surmount that obstacle. She jumps, and like Chauncy, she ignores the lovely soft, warm, squishy dog bed she has been provided, much to my consternation. It's red and black and decorated with bears. I love it. She ignores it. Right now she's lying on the heating grate.

"Get in the bear bed kitten!" She just looks at me.

I bought three jingle balls yesterday. God only knows where they are now. But boy does she love playing with paper. A paper bag, a movie receipt, my paper pirate, a gift card - doesn't matter, it's paper.

So the kitten is now five months old. Basically she's a ten year old with ADHD. I've found the following things to be true:

• The minute I walk in the door I better pick her up and pay attention to her or else she will do something spiteful like pee on my bed.

• Her obscene fascination with water has graduated to the toilet, even when I'm using it. Kitten! There is nothing more disconcerting than sitting on the throne having your morning constitutional and feeling a furry body try to squeeze between the back of the porcelain and your ass. KITTEN, WHAT ARE YOU DOING?!

• She now wants to hunt her dry food, as well as hunt her water. "You have food in your bowl, kitten. Get out of the cat food bag!" You were ignoring the bag before. Okay, this is one thing Chauncy did do, but he was a pig.

• The running is getting faster and the jumps are getting higher. I am also convinced the kitten is part ferret. She has these huge rabbit legs she hasn't quite grown into yet, which result in a ferret war dance when she gets all worked up. She jumps and hops and sometimes her back feet take over, sending her tipping ass over tea kettle. Today, as I was getting ready to leave for my temp job, she jumps on the dining room table, then onto the suitcase and finally leaps at the chandelier! KITTEN! WHAT ARE YOU DOING? She nearly caught it, though what she would have done hanging there is beyond me. I mean, that light fixture is seven feet in the air. For a critter that's only 6" high, that is a long ass way to fall.

• Early morning face sitting. If I move, she appears and falls on my face. Chauncy was never a face sitter. I remove her and she comes back. It's a game. Did I mention she was also snogging my bunny slippers? That was way weird.

• She's starting to stalk. She stalks her tail, bottle caps, wine corks, dust bunnies, all sorts of invisible things I can't see. She pounces, leaps back and runs away like her ass is on fire. Sometimes she jumps on the stuffed squirrel and tries to eviscerate him with her huge back rabbit feet. That does my heart good.

• She will chew on you, but she won't bite. I am waiting for the day that she's too big and fat to get into the little places where I can't reach her.

• She's a critic. She wanted some of what I was eating. It wasn't meat or fish, it was a rice cake. I knew she wouldn't like it. She sniffed at a piece then tried to bury it. Hey, it's not that bad.

• She plays fetch with many things; the multi colored toy my friend Krystal gave her or one of the ornaments she took off the tree. She will trot around with them hanging out of her mouth, looking very pleased with herself. Great, you killed it, now go eat the ants that have showed up in the bathroom to steal your water.

• She is many things, but boring isn't one of them and the soft cuteness goes a long way. It's a defense mechanism for crazy kittens. I think it keeps us from eating them. Well, except for the Chinese. They eat anything, and I do mean anything, but that is another tale for another day.

I was going to post this on Facebook, but my sister is lurking there, and the last thing I need is for my sister to get wind that I have another cat. I don't even think the niece and nephew know their cat cousin died a year and a half ago. Not that they really care that much. They want a human cousin. I told them they better be content with cousins of the cat and dog variety because that is all they are getting. Auntie has no husband and anyway her eggs are stale.

Then came the time to put up the Christmas tree. I switched to a fake tree about five years ago and I love it. It looks nice, is six feet tall, has way paid for itself and (the best thing) already has pre-strung lights. Chauncy always ignored the tree. He ignored the ornaments. He could have cared less. The kitten is part monkey. She gets up inside and climbs the tree. Did I mention she has thumbs? Yes, the polydactel business. Having thumbs only adds to the climbing crazies.

She climbs as high as she can and bats at the ornaments. I only decorated with wood, plastic, metal or paper ornaments this year and left any ceramic or glass ones in the box. I know I need to get a squirt bottle. I've been trying to spray her with a bottle of spray olive oil but that can get messy, and it makes her harder to catch when she's all greasy.

All of this does allow for hours of amusement. Beth and Andy refuse to give up their mantra that, "She was the quiet one!" Yeah and I'm Pam Anderson! Last night as she was lounging at the top of the tree, I tossed a bottle cap from my beer on the floor as a lure. Alia dove off and ran down the outside of the six foot high tree, practically flying in her haste to get at the bottle cap. The wooden sheep ornament took a nose dive as she barreled over it.

"WHAT ARE YOU DOING?"

On the First Day of Christmas some Germans gave to me, a kitten in a fake tree...

DIETING, EXERCISE AND WHY CAN'T YOU JUST RUN AROUND THE HOUSE

This morning dawned chill with the realization that my ass just acquired its own zip code. This is unacceptable. I've always had a great ass, but I suppose all that mayonnaise had to camp out somewhere for the winter. I guess I'm lucky it wasn't in my arteries. So, I decided I need to diet and exercise more. However I have this weird thing about exercising, which is also why I think Americans don't do it more.

1) It's hard
2) It's sweaty
3) It takes time
4) It's hard

I know, I have my Wii Fit, which I like, but it mocks me. I was determined to work out every day with it so I could get below the mocking threshold. Problem? It takes so much time. I get up between 4:45 and 5am in the morning so I don't have to rush and will be able to leave the house at 6:30 for work. I tried to do a 30 minute work-out in the morning but discovered that after turning the unit on, going through all the talking and the weighing and the transitions between games, the 30 minute workout took near an hour to complete. That didn't leave me enough time in the morning.

Then, when I get home from my contract job around 6:15pm, if there is no traffic, I've got to make dinner, give the Abomination some attention and try to clean up a bit, which doesn't leave a lot of time. Time is the enemy of lard asses the world over.

I also wanted to work out and lose some weight before getting back on the WiiFit because I'm scared; scared of the scale and the mocking and the fact that it's a stupid piece of plastic. The scale doesn't get that I don't eat crap or drink soda, but I can't go off the pill or I will burst into flame twelve times a day, just like Liz Sherman from Hellboy. I really can't deal with that. This reminds me of cleaning the house before the cleaning lady comes over, so she won't think you're a slob.

So, I've found a solution – Lent. Yes the Catholic holiday of guilt and penance and focusing on how much better my fiancé is than just about everyone else on the planet. I asked the big JC what he thought about giving up booze and take up dieting for Lent. He laughed and made himself a Brandy and Soda because it's the drink of Kipling. Then he watched American Idol and mocked Simon's hair. I'm not so sure marrying Jesus is a good thing.

Anyway, I decided to go back on the Atkins diet for Lent. No, I'm not Catholic but why let that stop me? The Induction phase of this plan is as close to Hell as I'm going to get this side of perdition. I did consider joining a gym and having a trainer yell at me – I mean MOTIVATE me but who has the money for a gym and a trainer?

Then it hit me – umm, can't you run for free? Can't you walk for free? Can't you jog around the house while picking up heavy cans and going up and down the back stairs until you want to puke and all that for... FREE?

What did people do for exercise before gyms and trainers and pilates and buns of steel DVDs? They worked. They lifted and carried and walked and ran and threw things. As a kid I could ride my bike all over the neighborhood all afternoon and never get tired. Now? I'm tired LOOKING at a bike.

I'm serious, Lent it is! Now, of course, if there was a special occasion then I would have to make an exception. Hey, the Catholic Church did. Lent is supposed to be 40 days, but it's not. It's 46 days, because the church doesn't count Sundays so that means six more days of penance. I look at it like this. You get six free days during Lent to fall off the wagon. Lent is 40 days – screw this extra six days crap – now I have a buffer. This sounds completely doable.

My new ass will let you know how this works out.

MY BIG, LOUD, IRISH-JEWISH MARRIAGE

I had a banner day on April 1st. I decided to marry my fiancé, Jesus Christ, or the Big JC as we call him around the house. I was very excited, especially by the cost savings for wine at the reception. I mean when your hubby can provide wine and food for everyone, who needs a caterer? This also means, with the wine, liqueur, food and cake taken care of, I had more to spend on a dress. If you have seen some of those designer dresses, you know they are not cheap. Well, some are, but not in the financial sense. I mean honestly, have you seen the Pnina Tornai transparent, corset-style wedding gowns? I know strippers, pole dancers or stripping pole dancers for that matter, need dresses too but daaamn.

Don't worry, my dress was wonderful and sexy and elegant and never seen on this planet before. I mean what is the point of marrying a God if you do it in a dress that any mere mortal can purchase at your local bridal shop?

Unfortunately, it didn't last long; the marriage, not the dress. I didn't actually make it to the ceremony, let alone the reception. I called the wedding off. I know, I suck. What the hell is wrong with me? I will date total losers for years, wasting my time and my life, but I break it off with the Son of God? Yeah, it sounds kinda bad when you put it that way.

Now, don't be getting all mad at Jesus. It wasn't his fault. I mean, he's perfect. He provided an endless stream of wine, Sangria and gin on request. We could feed large crowds at dinner parties with no problem and let me tell you that the walking on water thing is great for winning money at bars.

It wasn't Mary Magdalene either. She's a Saint. Literally. No, honestly, she's a sweetie and makes the best snickerdoodle cookies. She has no problem sharing.

The problem was... the nuns. In the end, I just couldn't get past the old, dried up, no humor, Irish nuns. They were just a whole basket of buzz kill. I told JC that he needed to dump those women, especially Sister Mary Margaret who used to chase after me when I was in 8th grade. It wasn't like I really did anything wrong. We were kids for Christ sake! We would just parade past her classroom windows on the way to the pool for PE and flash our bikinis at her 4th grade boys. Jesus, give me a break. No really, Jesus, give me a break and break up with this pain in my ass but no, he owed her. They were all so dedicated, they married him first, blah, blah, blah.

So I decided to let JC out of the contract. We just went back to the way things were. I mean he's a great guy but the nuns... no way Jay. It's me, it's all me. I am a solitary creature and all that company is just a little much.

By the way, in case anyone is interested, I asked JC about the whole gay marriage thing and guess what? He's all for it. He said, my Father made gays, straights, trannies, and all sorts of flavors on this Earth, and he doesn't make mistakes. Just having one flavor of ice cream, even if it's a great one like Caramel Almond Toffee Crunch, gets boring if that is all you get forever. Variety is what makes us great. So there it is. Get married, have fun, make love responsibly and don't feel guilty.

Honestly, those kill joys that were kicked out of England and landed on Plymouth Rock have been dead for a long time. WHY are people still listening to them? They weren't tolerant people. They didn't have a love-in with the native inhabitants of this country. They were religious fanatics who were not wanted in their own country. They had zero tolerance for anyone that didn't look like them or think the same way they did.

Please don't use the Puritans as role models.

THE ANGRY COW, MY THONG AND THE POLICE

I can't believe this is happening. This is kind of a two part story. First, Jason and Karrie came over for dinner Wednesday night. Splash Poo Mansion has been having its sewer lines replaced for the past two days (wow, too much poo over at Splash Poo I guess) and parking has been dicey. There is parking in the afternoon, but the streets fill up around 6:30pm, and with the equipment taking up space until 6pm, parking is a challenge.

They were supposed to arrive around 7pm, so I went outside and moved my car back towards Splash Poo Mansion's driveway so Jason could park across my driveway. Jason calls at 7pm to let me know that Karrie is stuck in traffic and they will be late. I keep glancing out the window to make sure no moron takes a hankerin' to parking in that spot. Sure enough, here must be something in the air because the morons sniff out my bare patch of parking real estate – right across my driveway.

So, here I am yet again, hanging out my window, yelling that my Marine boyfriend is coming home any minute in a bad temper, and they need to move their car with all due haste so he can park there. Why even mention this latest example of rude and illegal behavior on the part of the local citizenry? Is it of life or death importance? It's not, except The Cow overheard me and got a heads up that I was having company.

As I've mentioned, I'm a good neighbor. I don't have loud parties, I'm not inconsiderate. I don't get drunk, take off all my clothes and

245

run down the street screaming, "I'm a cheeseburger, I'm a cheeseburger!" Well, there was that one time in college, but that doesn't count now. I'm older now and wiser and slower.

Jason and Karrie finally show up. We have a nice dinner, go through two bottles of wine and then I brought out the bottle of Rosa Regale (the Italian champagne that tastes like roses). I don't know when The Cow put the flasher in the window. I don't know if Jason or Karrie noticed it. We were too busy eating and drinking and looking at vacation pictures that resemble houses of ill repute. They left after midnight, and I decided to watch a little TV while nibbling on the remains of our pig dinner. I was just minding my own business when there it was... "flash, flash, flash." Doesn't this woman have a life? Evidently not.

When I got up at 3am to get some water, I turned on the lights in the dining room and the kitchen (hey, I had to see) before turning them off and going back to bed. I realize she has a problem with me turning on any of my lights while she is slumbering in her Cow Cave, but I needed hydration so screw her.

Well, the next morning I am washing my delicate underthings and hanging them on the balcony rail like white trash because I just could not drag myself over to the laundromat. I realize I'm running the risk of another run-by underwear snatching by The Squirrel but I need clean knickers. Don't judge me. I figure my thongs had been out there about an hour when there was a knock on my door. I looked out the window to see two of Oakland's finest on my front porch. Yes, it was the police. WTF?

It seems The Cow called the cops because my knickers were hanging off my deck and, I don't know, she mistook them for a terrorist or a WMD or a killer squirrel. The nice policeman informed me they had received a complaint that I was discharging a firearm within the city limits and had suspicious items on my deck. I told them that my neighbor was in dire need of professional help and that while accidentally dropping an item off the balcony onto the cement might startle someone, I certainly wasn't shooting at anyone. I invited them in to see for themselves.

Yes, I took them out back and there were my thongs, waving in the breeze like Tibetan prayer flags. They agreed that my underwear was not a threat to Homeland Security, there was nothing suspicious on my property and they were sorry to have bothered me. Also, if this happened again, I could file a complaint against Bessie the Bovine (for wasting their time if nothing else.)

I contemplated telling the officers about the squirrels but didn't want them to change their good opinion of me or question my sanity, so off they went.

I am so wanting to boot that cow in the taco right now except she would bowl me over with her potent breath

EVERYBODY WANTS TO RULE THE WORLD

Especially William Henry Gates III, also know to his friends (Does he have friends?), as Bill. Born into a well-off family, he dropped out of college and changed the face of the world for nerds everywhere. Everything started out so bright and shiny until the crushing of competition and the human spirit, until the monopolies and the shitty products. Vista? WHY?

Bill, why do you keep shipping out buggy crap when you know it's buggy crap? I know, because you can and now Bill gives hope to the jobless, huddled masses that can code. Microsoft has announced that there are jobs! Yes, if you can work in IT – Bill has a well paying job for you. In fact, Microsoft is dying to hire you. All you have to do is send in your resume. There's only one catch. No, you don't have to move to India but close. You have to move to Fargo, North Dakota.

My mother was born in Wishek, North Dakota. I've been to Fargo. It's nothing to write home about. North Dakota is basically a shit hole with snow. Sorry people from North Dakota. I will say it's tons better than Wyoming. North Dakota is like New York compared to Wyoming. 98% of the ugliest people on the planet live in Wyoming, but that's another topic.

Let it just be said, North Dakota is a barren wasteland both visually and culturally. Face it, there are fewer than 700,000 people in the whole state! There are more people than that in Orange County alone. But then, people want to live in California. Even with us sliding into financial ruin, we still have sea, surf, sand, snow, mountains, gourmet food, culture and great weather. We'll soon all be living in tents, but hey, the Native Americans did it for eons before we killed them and stole their land, so we should be able to figure it out. If not, the stupid will die off leaving more for the rest of us.

Microsoft is an interesting company to work for. I've known Microsoft engineers that get bat shit crazy when they're on deadline, They barricade themselves in their offices, subsisting on Jolt Cola, Cheetos and any flat food that can be slipped under the door on a sheet of paper (usually processed cheese food slices).

You think I'm kidding? I'm not. Here's a prime example. Last night, an old friend of mine from the tech industry stopped by. I'll call him "Adam" as he was the first guy to show me how to code. He arrived on my doorstep in a frenzy of eight-year-old girl shrieking hysteria. Sorry, that makes him sound too much like a weenie (which he is) and I promised I would always support his attempts at masculine virility. So let's back up for a moment. He showed up on my doorstep, hammered on the door, stated authoritatively that he needed to see me, tossed back some whiskey and moseyed into the room. Do people still mosey? Anyway, he really did sound like an eight-year-old girl at a High School Musical screening. I felt pity for him and thought the Abomination could do with working her ferret war dance magic on a new victim, so I let him in. After all, there have been no pee incidents since Jason and Kristen came over on Sunday night and she piddled on a bag.

Adam had a problem. It seems his company is working on some new, super secret... thingy that I can't talk about, but let's just say this. We all know from Star Trek: The Next Generation that if the halo deck was for real, we would never leave our houses and the world would end. Well boys and girls, prepare, the end is near! Did I say that? No, that was some Revelations Bible nut. Ignore me.

Anyway, he had a big work problem that involved various lines of code, bug hunting, Big Concepts, Buy In and I think some C++ thrown in for good measure. I tried to learn C++ many years ago and it eluded me, since it involved more mathematical concepts than my brain was able to comprehend. I always thought Algebra was bullshit but not with C++ in the 1990's. I'm sure the interface has changed some since then, but I was scared off and ran back to my XML, HTML and my beloved DOS that gets no love anymore.

I'm losing you aren't I?

What does this have to do with Bill Gates and engineers run amok? Not a great deal. I was just pondering the oddities of the universe and how they intersected with my life. I loved my career in the tech industry even with the crushing deadlines and the whacky behavior. There was so much creative energy. I just can't picture having beer bashes, team building trips to play Bocce ball or Nerf gun fights in Fargo. I could be wrong. I'm sure there are many 40 year old virgins, who have never seen a grown woman naked, who will jump at this opportunity and I say, "Good for you!"

In the end, Adam didn't explode, which was a good thing since I have a new couch. I made him a Batcave martini, which calmed him down. He then wanted to watch "The Secret of Roan Innish." As we sipped our drinks, the Abomination climbed to the very top of the "now past the appointed time for Holidays" tree, grabbed my bunny angel in her fist of a paw and threw it off the tree. That move just seemed to say, "I am Queen of the tree and all of you pathetic monkeys are my minions!"

Let's just hope Bill Gates doesn't give her a job, or we are all dead.

I'M PAM ANDERSON IN WYOMING

We all know by know that I've made some bad decisions in my personal life. If I could give you one piece of advice, it would be this. Listen to the voices in your head. I'm not talking about the loud, drunken ones you hear all the time. I'm talking about the small, whispery ones. Like the one that usually is accompanied by a feeling of "this is wrong" before the loud, drunken voices stomp all over it. Those loud voices are the devil on your shoulder; the small, whispery one is the angel. The angel won't lead you wrong. That whispery voice is your better self. It's the part of yourself that sees into the future and is so often ignored because its dreams are too large, its warnings too dire or its tastes too pedantic.

I'm here to tell you, ignore that voice at your own peril. Am I going crazy? No, not really. I just started thinking about men in my life who are now dead to me and how that happened. Yeah, some were out right evil people. Some made stupid choices or habitually lied to me, but I chose to be with them against the better judgment of the whispery voice.

The loud voice would say, "Well this one is better than the last one so that's something!" or "This one is better in bed than the last one. He was boring. That's something!" or "I know he really is a better person deep down." All of those are BAD reasons. The loud voice is lying to you. The loud voice is the easy voice. It tells you the easy path, strewn with puppies and kitties and cute wee hedgehogs.

You should never choose something just because it's easy. You should never settle for something the whispery voice says is not good enough for you. Eventually you will turn over the rock and find a predator, an abusive jerk, a narcissist or just that asshat who runs off with the trashy crack whore. They are all the same. Not good enough for you so don't sell yourself short.

I thought living in Northern California would increase my opportunities to meet men who weren't brainwashed by the Los Angeles, plastic, shallow, youth culture. I'm still waiting, or perhaps I am paying my penance for the horrid mistakes I made in the past.

I do know one thing. In Wyoming, I'm Pam Anderson! You see, I was on a road trip a few years back and I discovered something. The ugliest women live in Wyoming. I'm sorry, if you are the exception, good for you. I'm sure you have a husband and I don't, so you can feel smug now, but for the most part - yeah. Now it's true, I only saw women in the finest truck stops, diners and local watering holes. I was not up in the rich enclave of Jackson Hole, home of the Sundance Film Festival and the Sundance Kid himself, Robert Redford.

Nope, I was in regular Wyoming and I have one question. Did these women eat a ton of sweets as kids? Because most of them are missing teeth. These women fell out of the ugly tree and hit every branch on the way down. I got stares from the majority of the male population everywhere we went. It was like they were all giant parrots trying to make me part of their harem, now that I think about it.

I can hear you all now. You're saying, "Well then why don't you just move to Wyoming?" I would if I was one of those women who just has to have a man or die. Personally, I'm too picky. I would rather live as a "born again virgin" with my insane kitten and be eternally engaged to Jesus than ever fall down that rabbit hole again.

Then I started thinking, if there is a section of the population, even if it's in Wyoming, that thinks I'm Pam Anderson, perhaps there is hope for me yet. I could be Sandra Bullock in Concord or Reese Witherspoon in San Jose or Kathy Griffin in San Francisco. Now THAT gives me hope.

Hey, it could happen!

SEXY, SINGLE AND WELL-HEELED

Tonight is the crowning glory of female and gay man obsession the world over. It's the pinnacle of all types of girl empowerment and just an awesome piece of creative inspiration. Tonight is the premiere of the <u>Sex in the City</u> movie.

I admit I wasn't a fan from the beginning. I had heard about the show, but I didn't get HBO. One day my good friend Nicole sat me down in front of her television and introduced me to the DVD of <u>Sex in the City - Season 1</u>. Now that I think about it, this is how many things have worked out. Nicole introduced me to cool movies like <u>Drop Dead Gorgeous</u>, great shows like <u>Sex in the City</u> and fabulous artists like P!nk. How could I go wrong?

Well, after the first episodes I was hooked. I had to watch them all. They took up the majority of the spaces on my Netflix queue. My kitten was having to jump higher, hide longer and get into more trouble just to get my attention.

So now, with all of the characters and storylines fresh in my mind, Nicole and I were meeting our friend Kris and making a night of it. We got all tricked out in our fabulous dresses and shoes. We decided our "theme" was "looking for Carrie" because every good party needs a theme, just ask a gay man.

Nicole was Samantha, Kris was Miranda (as the most practical among us) and I was Charlotte (though I am not very much the "sweet/wants to be married" kind of person). I did have a nice cute pink dress and some fabulous Steve Madden pumps. Nicole, of course, wore leopard print and had a huge purse. I think she could have stowed the entirety of Samantha's toy collection in there.

We had dinner at a French eatery right down the street from the theater and, with pre-purchased tickets in hand, proceeded to stuff ourselves on snails, fish and all manner of French delicacies. Of course we had to have drinks as well. I mean, what kind of <u>Sex in the City</u> girls would we be without cocktails? I think the only thing that would have made our experience perfect would have been if we had a couple of fabulous gay men to share our cocktails with.

Once we were in the theater, we seated ourselves in the bottom row of the middle of the stadium seating. You know, you walk into the theatre, the seats are all raked upwards and there is a large walkway? You can go down into the seats where you are right next to the screen or you can climb up into the "Gods" to watch from under the projector. Our seats were by the area for a wheelchair and that person's party. Well since there were no wheelchairs at this showing we took those seats and had a football field of room in front of us. In fact we didn't have any close neighbors due to the empty sections on either side of the set of three seats for the aforementioned wheelchairs. It was perfect.

I looked around and saw the audience was made up of 70% women, 20% gay men and 10% sulky straight men who had been dragged there by their women. You know there were only going along with the program so they would get laid afterwards. This was a perfect evening, but Nicole had other plans to put this night over the top. As the lights went down, she reached into her huge purse and pulled out martini glasses and handed two to Kris and I. She then reached back into the bag, which I was convinced by this time was bottomless, and pulled out chilled bottles of pink liquid secreted in Crystal Geyser bottles. She poured them into our glasses. As the movie started to roll, we toasted each other, sat back and sipped our Cosmos. This was the best thing ever. We were together, we were fabulous and everything was right with the world.

Well, if this book was a movie, our heroine would loop back around to the beginning and all the issues she had would be resolved. I would have my life back. I would have a great job I loved, a solid relationship and a secure future. All would be rosy and bright. Our heroine would be redeemed. Unfortunately, life is not a movie and at this part in my story, I don't have a job. I don't have a relationship and a secure future of any kind seems very far off.

However, one of my favorite literary survivors, Scarlett O'Hara, said it best. "Tomorrow is another day." I may not have a job, I may not have a house for much longer but I do have a great life. My job has become sharing my experiences with the masses. My long term relationship is with myself, and that's a challenge, let me tell you. One of my friends once said, "You have a friendly face and a nice smile. I'm sure most people who don't know you, think you are friendly and approachable by just glancing at you. You don't look downtrodden and dramatic. Until, we get to know you and we learn you are like a blender with its lid off."

It's true. I am a whirling blender. So for now I think I need to be my first priority. All those men can take a number, except for Alan Rickman, I'll take his calls. I have a fabulous family and great friends. I'm sure with their support I will even hunt down that evil squirrel one day. Perhaps I'll open a couture millinery renowned for its intricate fascinators fashioned from the finest wee squirrel pelts. It could happen.

To quote from one of my favorite films, "No man is poor who has friends." Well, move over George Bailey because I just may be the richest woman in San Francisco.

ABOUT THE AUTHOR

Deirdre Sargent was born in San Francisco where as a child, she learned to charm the nice Italians out of snow cones. She has a degree in theatre arts and is a graduate of the American Academy of Dramatic Arts - West. She has been involved in theatre since she was eight including performing with the California Shakespeare Festival.

Deirdre has been writing since college even if it was mainly on dressing room walls. Her style tends towards the humorous and irreverent, however she is also a huge Disney fan. She is the author of the Mouse Moments series, an extensive collection of Disney guidebooks filled with her unique brand of humor.

She lives in the Bay Area with her huge Maine Coon cat Alia aka The Abomination, an antique bar filled with premium liquor and her collection of Xbox games.

OTHER TITLES

Mouse Moments Travel Guide Series:
  A Humorous Guide Through The Magic Kingdom
  A Humorous Guide Through Disneyland
  A Humorous Guide Through Disney's Animal Kingdom –
  Coming for Fall 2012

Follow me on Facebook: Deirdre A. Sargent
http://DeirdreSargent.com for blogs, books and appearances